MOZART

PIANO CONCERTO IN C MAJOR, K. 503

The Score of the New Mozart Edition

Historical and Analytical Essays

NORTON CRITICAL SCORES

BACH CANTATA NO. 4
edited by Gerhard Herz

BACH CANTATA NO. 140
edited by Gerhard Herz

BEETHOVEN SYMPHONY NO. 5 IN C MINOR
edited by Elliot Forbes

BERLIOZ FANTASTIC SYMPHONY
edited by Edward T. Cone

CHOPIN PRELUDES, OPUS 28
edited by Thomas Higgins

DEBUSSY PRELUDE TO "THE AFTERNOON OF A FAUN"
edited by William W. Austin

MOZART PIANO CONCERTO IN C MAJOR, K. 503
edited by Joseph Kerman

MOZART SYMPHONY IN G MINOR, K. 550
edited by Nathan Broder

PALESTRINA POPE MARCELLUS MASS
edited by Lewis Lockwood

PURCELL DIDO AND AENEAS
edited by Curtis Price

SCHUBERT SYMPHONY IN B MINOR ("UNFINISHED")
edited by Martin Chusid

SCHUMANN DICHTERLIEBE
edited by Arthur Komar

STRAVINSKY PETRUSHKA
edited by Charles Hamm

WAGNER PRELUDE AND TRANSFIGURATION from *TRISTAN AND ISOLDE*
edited by Robert Bailey

A NORTON CRITICAL SCORE

Wolfgang Amadeus Mozart

PIANO CONCERTO IN C MAJOR
K. 503

The Score of the New Mozart Edition
Historical and Analytical Essays

Edited by
JOSEPH KERMAN
UNIVERSITY OF CALIFORNIA AT BERKELEY

W · W · NORTON & COMPANY
New York · London

Library of Congress Catalog Card No. 78-90991

W. W. Norton & Company, Inc., 500 Fifth Avenue, New York, N.Y. 10110

ISBN 0-393-09890-7

PRINTED IN THE UNITED STATES OF AMERICA

0

Contents

Introduction

The Work—Ever since the earliest days of concert-giving in the modern sense—that is, since the time of Mozart—concertos have been solidly entrenched in symphony programs. This popularity is not hard to explain. One of the deepest and most immediate of audience responses rests on the age-old fascination in personal virtuosity, which the concerto serves in the grandest possible arena. Understandably, perhaps, a form which depends on instrumental virtuosity has gained the reputation of occupying a lower plane of musical excellence than do other types of instrumental music, such as the symphony or sonata or string quartet. Until recently concertos were often composed by star performers who would not have ventured to write symphonies or operas, and even in today's repertory there are many familiar concertos in which the element of virtuoso display is overindulged. As a consequence, it has sometimes been felt that concertos in general, including even those by the greatest composers, are bound to compromise musical values with considerations of a more sensational, crowd-pleasing nature. The form itself has been open to charges of showiness and lack of substance.

Sir Donald Tovey's famous essay on *The Classical Concerto* (1903), reprinted in this volume, set out to demolish this notion and demonstrate the unique esthetic possibilities available to the concerto form. The example Tovey used was Mozart's Piano Concerto in C major, K. 503. And since the time that Tovey wrote, Mozart's piano concertos have certainly come to form an exception to the strictures suggested in the above paragraph. For most musicians, they occupy a special place not only within the concerto repertory as a whole, but also within Mozart's large and varied output. Mozart's own delight in the form is shown by the great number of examples he composed and by the care and variety he lavished on them: he composed 23 in all, 15 of them in his mature period, the period beginning with his move to Vienna in 1781 and ending with his death ten years later. Twelve concertos can be regarded as masterpieces—a considerably greater number than can be claimed by any other composer of his or any other period. The mere size of this repertory has contributed to the respect in which it is held. Over and above this, however, there has been a growing appreciation of Mozart's particular sensitivity in grasping and manipulating the qualities inherent in the concerto, qualities which have their own integrity and power distinct from those of other musical genres.

The Concerto in C major, K. 503, is one of the latest of the great Vienna works. It was the one concerto written for the concert season 1786–87, which also saw the "Prague" Symphony and the two magnificent String Quintets in C and G minor; *Don Giovanni* followed later in 1787. In the previous season, 1785–86, Mozart had produced *The Marriage of Figaro* and the three famous piano concertos in E-flat major, A major, and C minor. The composition of the Concerto in C is recorded in Mozart's own meticulous catalogue of his works under the date December 4, 1786, and he seems to have played the piece at a concert on the very next day.[1] (Most of Mozart's concertos were written for his own use at such concerts, or "academies.") Soon afterwards, several other performances can be traced; this is not the case with any of the other concertos, and it suggests that the C-major work made a special impression, no doubt on account of its grand scale. Only a few months after the first performance, a student of Mozart named Marianne Willmann gave an academy featuring one of his concertos; it is not said which, but the C major is considered to be the most likely. Then in March 1789, Mozart's "big concerto in C" was played at Dresden by another of his students, a much more important one, Johann Nepomuk Hummel. At that time an infant prodigy of nine years, Hummel lived to become one of the most celebrated pianists and composers of the early 19th century; among his many compositions are decorated versions of the slow movements and cadenzas for Mozart concertos (including this one). In May of the same year, Mozart himself, on a visit to Leipzig, played our concerto again at a lengthy concert devoted to his own music. Incidentally, one of Beethoven's first public appearances in Vienna in 1795 was as a soloist in an unspecified Mozart concerto. Considering the special popularity of the

1. Information in this paragraph is derived from Otto Erich Deutsch, *Mozart, A Documentary Biography* (see Bibliography).

Concerto in C, this may perhaps have been the one he played; it certainly has some Beethovenian features.

In modern times, the Concerto in C has not figured on concert programs as often as some of the others, such as the very fine Concertos in A major (K. 488), D minor (K. 466), and C minor (K. 491). The two latter concertos, Mozart's only two examples in the minor mode, have enjoyed special popularity since Romantic times on account of their stormy, pathetic, and even tragic character. But it is probably safe to say that none of Mozart's concertos is performed as frequently as one might expect from their reputation, to say nothing of their worth. Few pianists are able to do justice to Mozart, and only a certain type of pianist is willing to forego the easier effects of power and brilliance to be obtained with 19th- and 20th-century concertos. On the modern piano, Mozart's runs and arpeggios sound almost too easy and straightforward, too transparent—dangerously so for the player who concentrates on brilliant effects at the expense of subtler musical values. On the much more fragile piano of Mozart's time, Mozart's concertos sound as dazzling as do Bach's concertos on the harpsichord of Bach's time; but neither Bach nor Mozart is well served by the modern piano. There is also a problem with the balance—the balance of musical forces on which the whole idea of the concerto depends. If the large symphony orchestra of today is reduced to a point at which the filigree of Mozart's wind writing can sound well, the modern piano sounds too loud by comparison; the piano has to keep holding back, which goes against the fundamental spirit of the concerto "contest." If the symphony orchestra is not reduced, the contest can degenerate into an un-Mozartean battle royal.

In short, Mozart's piano concertos pose special performance problems that are not felt with his symphonies, quartets, or even his works for piano solo. The concertos are most successful in a chamber-orchestra situation, and with a soloist who has the double instincts of a chamber-music player and a virtuoso. It helps also if the conductor is blessed with the historical instinct—the instinctive ear for a sound-ideal which is no longer current, but has to be recreated in a new imaginative guise.

The Score—The score reprinted here is that contained in the new complete scholarly edition of Mozart's works, the *Neue Mozart-Ausgabe* (NMA). The Concerto in C is not one of those works which present particularly difficult or interesting textual problems; although the NMA edition is certainly to be regarded as the most authoritative available, it does not differ in major respects from other scores that the student is likely to encounter (Broude Brothers, Eulenburg). A *Textual Note* following the score mentions some of the more significant details that emerge from the editing of the concerto.

Classic concertos were of course designed to have cadenzas improvized at the end of the first movement (and also at other points in certain concertos—although not K. 503). Mozart wrote down his own improvized cadenzas for some of the works, but K. 503 is not among them. Cadenzas for his concertos do exist from the pens of various pianists not long after his death; there is, for instance, a set published in 1801 by a certain Philipp Karl Hoffmann, who could claim to have actually met Mozart. Hummel's popular cadenzas appeared around the same time. But taste was changing rapidly, as was also piano technique and indeed the physical instrument itself. Comparison with Mozart's own cadenzas, to say nothing of general musical considerations, shows that the cadenzas of Hoffmann and his contemporaries are dreadfully overblown—disproportionately long, full of figuration that is coarse and flashy, and marked by gratuitous thematic recapitulations and remote modulations. The cause of historical "authenticity" is not necessarily served by playing or reprinting cadenzas dating from close to Mozart's own time, and perhaps it is just as well that pianists who play K. 503 have not settled on any one particular cadenza for regular use. A number may be consulted in modern editions.[2]

It is also well-known that within the actual body of the concertos Mozart's score does not always indicate exactly what he meant to be played. With one concerto, indeed, the "Coronation" Concerto in D, K. 537, the piano part in Mozart's manuscript amounts to no more than a guide for his own memory—or improvisation—in performance.[2a] There are places in the fast movements of some other concertos (not K. 503) that require filling in with virtuoso material (for a notorious place of this kind, see the Concerto in B-flat, K. 595, mm. 161–62 and 322–23). But the problem is especially pressing with the slow movements, in which

2. Paul Badura-Skoda, *Kadenz zum 1. Satz des Klavierkonzert in C-dur, K. 503,* Doblinger, Vienna, c. 1956; Robert Casadesus, in the two-piano edition of the concerto by International Music Co., New York, 1951; Friedrich Gulda, *Kadenz zum 1. Satz des Klavierkonzert in C-dur, K.V. 503,* Doblinger, Vienna, c. 1957; A. E. Müller, *Kadenzen zu acht berühmten Mozart-Konzerten,* ed. Alfred Kreutz, Peters, Leipzig, c. 1959; Soulima Stravinsky, *Eighteen Cadenzas and Four Fermatas to Mozart's Piano Concerti,* Peters, New York, c. 1957.

2a. See facsimiles in Emanuel Winternitz, *Musical Autographs,* Princeton, 1955, repr. New York, 1965, vol. II, plates 75–80.

extensive improvised decorations were regularly employed.[3] Reprinted here are passages from the decorated version of the Andante of K. 503 by Ph. K. Hoffmann. Again, what Hoffmann played in 1801 is not necessarily a safe guide to what Mozart played in 1786, but in this area there is reason to believe that Hoffmann was not as far off as he was in his cadenzas. (The reader who is interested in this question should consult a decorated version of the Adagio of the Concerto in A, K. 488, published in the Critical Notes for the NMA [4]; the version is thought to stem from Mozart's time and perhaps even from Mozart's circle.) In any case, it seems clear that a performance of a concerto slow movement with no decorations at all would have struck Mozart and his contemporaries as a great peculiarity.

The Essays—In selecting historical and analytical essays dealing with the Concerto in C, the aim has been to include writings of some length and density, rather than a series of smaller notices. Two of the selections look inward in detail on the single work, while the other two look out from it toward Mozart's other concertos, and beyond them to the concerto at large. The essays are written from widely different (not to say hostile) points of view, which the reader should try to examine critically, reconcile, adopt, or reject.

The chapter on the piano concertos from *Mozart, His Character, His Work,* by Alfred Einstein, may be said to deal with the historical background in a double sense. Works by other composers are brought into consideration as influences on Mozart's earlier concertos; and the total series of Mozart's own concertos is presented as the most relevant "historical context" for a late masterpiece such as K. 503. Einstein's panoramic survey of Mozart's concerto output can be read with a good deal of interest even by those who do not know many of the works referred to. It is hoped indeed that the chapter will interest them in other concertos besides K. 503.

Tovey's *The Classical Concerto,* which has already been mentioned above, draws upon both history and analysis. But fundamentally the essay counts as a contribution to theory, the "theory" in this case being an exposition of the special conditions and requirements of the concerto

3. This matter was first discussed in a small book by the pianist and composer Carl Reinecke, who was noted for his Mozart playing, *Zur Wiederbelebung der Mozart'schen Clavier-Concerte,* Leipzig, 1891.

4. *Mozart: Neue Ausgabe sämtliche Werke, Kritische Berichte: Serie V, Konzerte, Lieferung 1. Werkgruppe 15: Klavierkonzerte, Band 7,* Kassel, 1964, pp. 10–14.

form. The analysis of K. 503, deliberately partial, is really there in order to illustrate the theory, which the student should be encouraged to consider—as Tovey does—in a broad historical context.

The climate of modern music study favors analysis on a much more detailed scale than was practiced by Tovey, but it is surprising how few such studies are to be found in print. The essay on K. 503 by Hans Keller follows the lead of Rudolph Réti, whose ideas have excited more interest and controversy in recent years than those of almost any other musical analyst. The present editor does not subscribe to Keller's system—rather the reverse—but believes that it deserves consideration both for its underlying attitudes and for its insights (if not for the way in which these are developed), and also as a corrective or supplement to other music-analytic points of view.

More conventional is the treatment of the last two movements of K. 503 by C. S. Girdlestone, from a book that goes through all of Mozart's twenty-three piano concertos in some detail. Girdlestone's descriptive analyses have been criticized by Keller and others, not without some reason, as insufficiently technical and overly impressionistic. The student must decide for himself whether Girdlestone's subjective efforts to get at the "feeling" of the music are more or less meaningful than Keller's supposedly objective analyses of musical unity.

Unfortunately, *Interpreting Mozart on the Keyboard,* by Eva and Paul Badura-Skoda, does not contain a directly relevant section that might have been included with these other essays. The book is strongly recommended for its discussion of the performance of Mozart's piano music in the light of historical evidence on the one hand, and a specifically modern musical sensibility on the other. It includes a section of fairly close comment on several of the concertos, but not on K. 503.

THE SCORE OF THE CONCERTO

Edited by

HERMANN BECK

ACKNOWLEDGMENT

This edition of Mozart's Piano Concerto in C major, K. 503, is printed by permission of Bärenreiter-Verlag Kassel-Basel-Paris-London from *W. A. Mozart, Neue Ausgabe sämtlicher Werke, herausgegeben in Verbindung mit den Mozart-Städten Augsburg, Salzburg und Wien von der Internationalen Stiftung Mozarteum Salzburg, Serie V, Werkgruppe 15, Band 7* (BA 4519), edited by Hermann Beck. The text of the *Neue Mozart-Ausgabe* has also been published by Bärenreiter in a separate score (BA 4742), a pocket score (TP 64), the complete performing materials (BS 4743), and the piano score (BA 4742a).

INSTRUMENTATION

1 Flute (*Flauto*)
2 Oboes
2 Bassoons (*Fagotti*)

2 Horns (*Corni*): in C in I and III, F in II
2 Trumpets (*Trombe*) in C
Timpani in C, G

Piano solo (*Klavier*)

Violin I
Violin II
Viola
Violoncello
Double Bass

PIANO CONCERTO IN C MAJOR, K. 503

17
p
24
f
a2
f
f
f
f
f
f
f
f
f
f

29
34

39
a 2
43

47
p
p
p
p
54
p
p
p
p
p
p

60
66
f
f
f
f
f
f
f
f
f
f
p
p
p

72
p
p
p
p
p
78
p
p
p
p
p
p

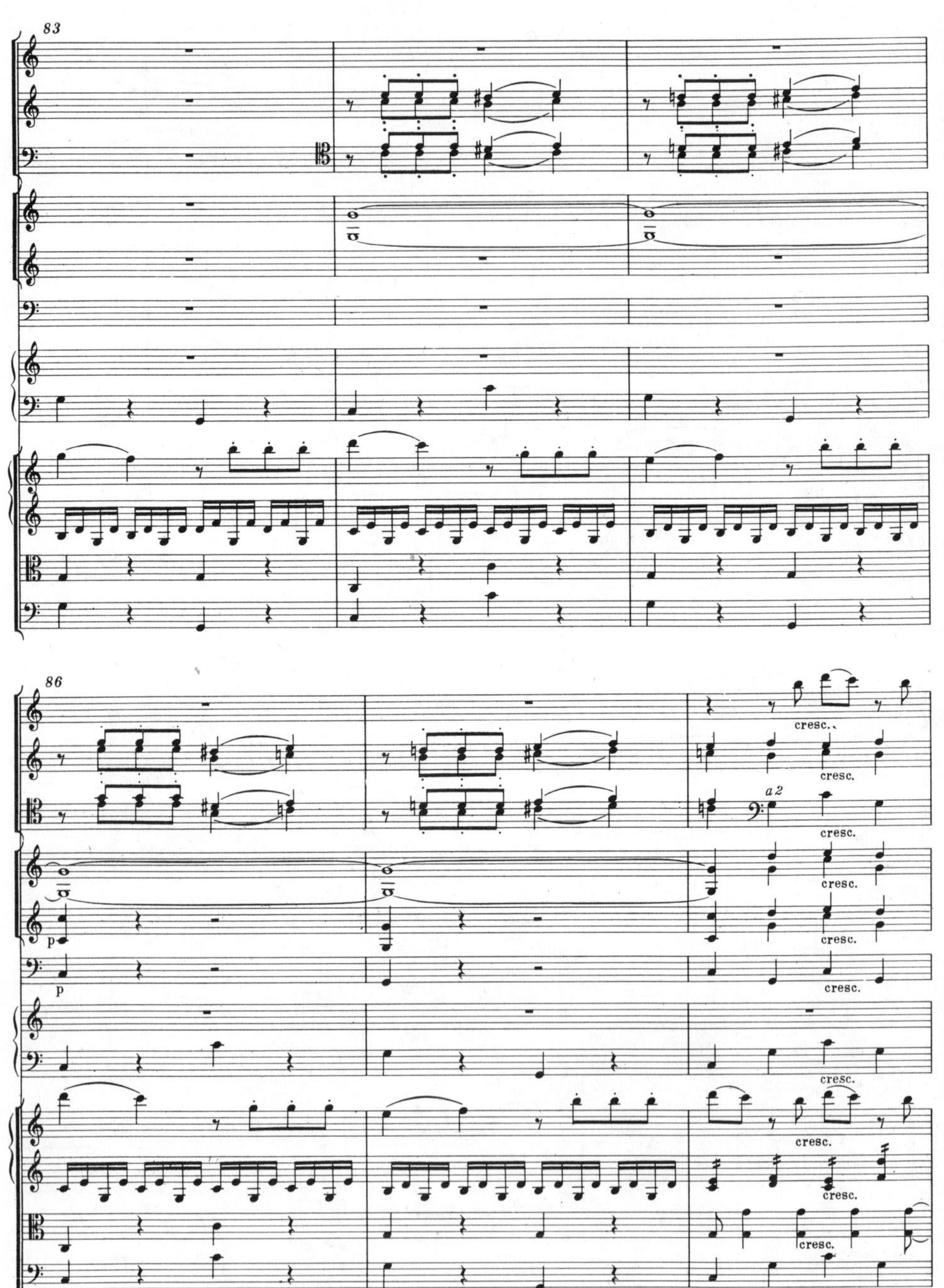
83
86
cresc.
a 2
p

89
f
p
tr
3
96

102
106
p

110
a2
f
116
tr
p

122
p
128

132
6
6
3
136

139
p
p
p
143
f
a 2
f
f
f
f
f
f
f
f
f

149
tr
155
p
mf

160
163

166
169
6

174
Violoncello
178
Bassi

182
Violoncello
Bassi
186

190
tr
194
tr
tr

199
tr
tr
tr
203

207
tr
212
cresc.
tr
tr
cresc.
f
f
a 2
f
cresc.
f
f
f
f
f
f
f
f

216
220

224
p
p
p
p
230
p

236
3
p
242

248
f
a 2
p
255

261
p
p
p
p
265

269
273

277
280

284
288
cresc.
a 2
f

* By analogy with mm. 124–25.

307
310

313
6
6
6
3
316
p
p

320
f
a 2
325
tr
330

335
p
p
p
p
340

344
349
Violoncello

353
p
p
p
Bassi
357
Violoncello

361
p
364
p
p
p
tr
Bassi

369
373

377
tr
tr
tr
382
tr
tr
tr

386
390

393
tr
398
cresc.
tr
tr
cresc.
f
f
f
a 2
f
cresc.
f
f
f
f
f
f
f

* Cadenza: see p. x.

413
p
419
p
p
p
p
p
p
p
p
p
p

424
428
a 2
cresc.
f
p

Andante
Flauto
Oboi
Fagotti
Corni in Fa/F
Klavier
Violino I
Violino II
Viola
Violoncello e Basso
p
sf
7

12
p
cresc.
sf p
f
p
tr
f
p
cresc.
14
f
sf p
sf
p
cresc.

16
tr
p
f
21
mf p
3

28
32
3

38
tr
44
tr

46
tr
tr
50
tr
tr

54

60
f
p
mfp
68

71
tr
tr
74
mfp
p
3
p
p
p
p

80
tr
85
tr
tr

88
90
tr
tr
tr
tr

94
98

100
3
tr
105
pp
pp
pp
3
pp
pp

Allegretto
Flauto
Oboi
Fagotti
Corni in Do/C
Trombe in Do/C
Timpani in Do, Sol / C, G
Klavier
Violino I
Violino II
Viole
Violoncello e Basso
p
6

16
24
f
a 2
tr

28
3
33
[♯]
[♮]
38

44
p
p
p
p
49

54
59
tr

64
p
p
p
69
3
3

74
Violoncelli
81
Bassi
staccati

86
91
p

96
101
p

106
p
111
ad libitum
a tempo

116
f
f
a 2
f
f
f
f
f
f
f
f
f
123
p
p
p

131
p
p
p
p
p
p
p
p
tr
141
p
p
tr
tr

149
p
p
p
p
155

162
f
f
f
f
f
f
f
f
f
f
f
p
169
p

175
p
Violoncello
181

186
p
Bassi
191
p

196
p
p
p
201

206

p

211

216
221

226
231
237
f
a 2
f
f
f
f
f
f
f
f

243
p
p
p
3
3
p
p
p
p
248
p

253
p
258

263
269
Violoncello

276
Bassi
staccati
280

284
Violoncelli
288

292
296

301
306

311
319
Bassi
Violoncelli

325
Bassi
331
tr
tr
p
p

336
tr
tr
tr
340

345
tr
tr
tr
p
p
350
tr

354
tr
360
sfp
sfp
sfp

364
p
p
368
tr

372
tr
f
a 2
cresc.
3
377

Textual Note

The score is one that was prepared in 1959 by Dr. Hermann Beck for the new complete scholarly edition of Mozart's works, the *Neue Mozart-Ausgabe* (NMA). The sources from which he worked were:

1. Mozart's original autograph score of 1786 (now in the Berlin State Library). This score is interesting in that, better than with most Mozart scores, the different shades of ink allow the researcher to tell just which sections or instrumental lines were written down first, and which others were filled in later (see the article by Gerstenberg cited in the Bibliography). Thus a study of this manuscript can yield some insight into Mozart's method of composition. In this autograph manuscript, the piano is clearly directed to play *col Basso* during the ritornellos, a direction which is rarely followed in modern performances, but which is of course followed in the NMA edition. It is also worth noting that in the autograph the finale is given no tempo indication.

2. A set of orchestral parts, without the solo, dating from 18th century and perhaps even from Mozart's lifetime (now in the great Abbey Library at Melk, lower Austria). Compared with the autograph score, these early orchestral parts show so many divergences of minor detail that it is clear they cannot have been copied directly from the autograph; they must have been copied from another score or other parts which are now lost, and which may well have been prepared or corrected by Mozart himself. Here it is interesting to see that some of the string parts are marked *Ripieno* and contain only the music of the tuttis. Also, at one point in the finale—which here is marked *Allegretto*—the parts have a slightly different version of the upward scales in the oboe and bassoon (mm. 247–49). Since this version avoids the parallel fifths between Bassoon II and the piano, Beck suspects that it may represent an improvement made by the composer; but he is not confident enough of this to put the improved version into the NMA edition.

3. Several published editions of orchestral parts from the years around 1800, one of them prepared under the direction of Mozart's widow Constanze (whose correspondence in the matter has been preserved).

Mozart, in his lifetime, had the opportunity to publish only a small portion of his music. When these early concerto editions were made, someone —not Mozart!—would have corrected any obvious slips of the pen in the manuscript they were working from, whether this was the original autograph or some other source derived from it; but they could have misjudged certain cases and they could well have introduced new slips of their own. Except in cases of clear error in the autograph, the latter is always more reliable than the early printed editions.

4. In addition, Beck scrupulously examined a dozen early 19th-century copies and editions, but found that since all of them were derived from the above sources, they added no new information of value.

In his Critical Notes (*Revisionsbericht*) to the edition, Beck describes all these sources in detail and lists several hundred places where the most important ones differ from one another. Most of the differences are very minor—ties and staccato dots left out, etc. It is worth noting that in the piano part of the old *Gesamtausgabe* score, reprinted by Broude Brothers, most of the longer legato slurs and all of the "legato" and "Ped." indications are inauthentic.

On page 65, this edition substitutes a II_2 chord in the piano left hand for the V_7 in the NMA, evidently an oversight on Mozart's part.

It is a principle of the *Neue Mozart-Ausgabe,* from which the present separate edition is reproduced, to indicate editorial additions in the score; in this connection the use of "a 2" in unison passages for pairs of wind instruments (engraved on one staff for the present edition) needs special explanation. The indication "a 2" is not to be regarded in the strict sense as an editorial addition, but simply as a rewriting of the instruments noted in the original on two staves. On these grounds the indication "a 2" is printed in normal and not in italic type.

Editorial additions and completions are given as sparingly as possible and are distinguishable as follows:

Letters (particularly dynamic and agogic signs) in italics.
Accidentals in square brackets.
Accents and dots in small print.
Phrasing in dotted lines.

The appendix to the NMA edition includes a facsimile and transcription of a few sketches by Mozart for the *Allegro maestoso,* which occur on a loose page with studies for the "Prague" Symphony in D, K. 504 (see pp. 102–4). The most interesting sketch concerns the opening sixteen-measure passage for the piano, mm. 96–112. In the autograph score Mozart originally wrote a simpler, ten-measure passage without any participation of the orchestra; but he crossed it out, used the sketch page to draft the present sixteen-measure passage, and then entered this, with a few more improvements, back on the autograph. There are two other small sketches for the solo part at mm. 208–14 and mm. 134–38, which do not differ significantly from the final version.

Decorated Version of the Andante *by Ph. K. Hoffmann*

Measures 1–12:

32
38
etc
Measures 58–86:

60
6
6
6
6
6
68
3
71
74

80
85
tr

Mozart's Sketches for the Allegro Maestoso

Original version of mm. 96–112, crossed out in Mozart's autograph manuscript:

Sketches on the sketch sheet:

[these measures indicated only roughly]
[mm. 134-138 and 312-316]
6
6
3
[sic!]

HISTORICAL AND ANALYTICAL ESSAYS

Unless specified otherwise, all numbered footnotes in the following essays are those of the author.

ALFRED EINSTEIN

The Synthesis: The Clavier Concerto †

Alfred Einstein (1880–1952) was one of the most important musical scholars of the early twentieth century. In Germany, prior to 1933, he was widely active in musicological ventures and also in the daily routine of music criticism; thereafter he lived in England, Italy, and America (after 1939). He was a cousin of Albert Einstein. Alfred's major works were an exhaustive study of the Italian madrigal of the sixteenth century, and an equally exhaustive revision of the famous Köchel catalogue, which is a listing of all Mozart's compositions in chronological order, together with full historical and bibliographical information about each one. The latter project involved Einstein in detailed examination of Mozart's manuscripts, letters, documents of the time, and quantities of contemporaneous music. Thus when he came to write a book on Mozart—he also wrote books on Schütz, Gluck, and Schubert—he was able to draw on more historical information, probably, than any other writer could command.

Einstein's great strength was working "in breadth" rather than "in depth"; it was not his way to plunge deeply into the analysis of individual works. When his comments on the concertos are not strictly historical, they are similar in nature to those of Girdlestone, whose book not surprisingly impressed Einstein (see p. 107).

Splendid as are the examples of the concerto form for string and wind instruments, it was only in the piano concertos that Mozart achieved his ideal. They are the peak of all his instrumental achievement, at least in the orchestral domain. Mozart cultivated the concerto for violin industriously, but only for a short time; to the concerto for single wind instruments—flute, oboe, bassoon, horn, clarinet—and the *sinfonia concertante,* he devoted only intermittent, though at times very serious, attention; but

† Chapter 17 of *Mozart, His Character, His Work,* by Alfred Einstein, transl. by Arthur Mendel and Nathan Broder.

with the piano concerto he concerned himself from earliest youth until the end, and undoubtedly we should have had more than just two piano concertos dating from the last four or five years of his life—we might have had ten or twelve such masterpieces—if the Vienna public had paid greater attention to Mozart than it did. For of course Mozart wrote no new concertos when he had no opportunity to play them. Of the more than fifty symphonies by Mozart there are, strictly speaking, four that belong among the eternal treasures of music; of the thirty-odd string quartets, ten. But among the twenty-three concertos for piano and orchestra, there is only one that is below the highest level—the concerto for three pianos (K. 242), written to be played not by Mozart himself or any capable soloist, but by three lady amateurs. One reason for the high quality of the piano concertos is the innate superiority of the piano over the other solo instruments, even when these instruments unite to form a *concertino* as in the *Sinfonia Concertante* for four wind instruments or the Double Concerto for violin and viola. Only in the piano concerto are two forces opposed that really balance each other, with neither one necessarily subordinate to the other. The piano is the only instrument that is not at a disadvantage either by reason of its limited tonal volume, like the violin, flute, or clarinet, or because of any limitations in respect to intonation and modulation, like the horn. It is just as powerful as the orchestra, to which it forms a worthy opponent because of the variety of tone production it possesses, as a highly developed percussion instrument. It should be remarked here again that Mozart wrote all his clavier works, including the concertos, not for the harpsichord but for the pianoforte, and that we should banish from the platform all those ladies and gentlemen who would like to claim the C minor Concerto, for example, or the C major, K. 503, for the harpsichord. We should also, of course, banish conductors who accompany a Mozart concerto with a string orchestra padded with ten double basses, forcing the pianist to produce a volume of tone that is possible only on our present-day mammoth instruments.

It was in the piano concerto that Mozart said the last word in respect to the fusion of the *concertante* and symphonic elements—a fusion resulting in a higher unity beyond which no progress was possible, because perfection is imperfectible. The penetrating monograph by C. M. Girdlestone, *Mozart et ses concertos pour piano* (Paris, 1939), rightly emphasizes the fact that the "emancipation of the orchestra," often attributed to Beethoven in his concerto-writing, was completely accomplished by Mozart. Beethoven perhaps juxtaposed the two forces more dramatically, and he pursued an ideal of virtuosity different from Mozart's; but at bottom he developed only one type among Mozart's concertos, which we may call for the present the "military" or "martial" type. Mozart's concerto form is a vessel of far richer, finer, and more sublime content. It is one of the perfections of Mozart's music that its dramatic element remains latent, and that it contains more profound depths than the struggle between opposing forces. Sometimes the contest in Mozart's works goes very far, but never so far that it could not be called a duality in unity. His piano concerto is really his most characteristic creation. It is the ideal and the realization of that which in some of his piano trios and in the two piano quartets fails of complete expression only because the piano in them is always the more powerful participant, and the strings always remain partially eclipsed by it. Mozart's piano concerto is the apotheosis of the piano—placing the instrument in the broad frame in which it belongs—and at the same time the apotheosis of the *concertante* element is embedded in the symphonic. Or one might even say: the symphonic element creates for itself a protagonist, the piano; it thus creates a dualism that endangers its unity; and then it conquers this danger. Mozart's piano concerto never seems to overstep the bounds of society music—how could it, since it was always intended for performance in public, and thus was prevented from having any quality of intimacy? And yet it always leaves the door open to the expression of the darkest and the brightest, the most serious, the gayest, the deepest feelings. It presses forward from the *galant* world into the symphonic; it lifts the listener to a higher level. Listeners who can really appreciate Mozart's piano concertos are the best audience there is.

Although we have said that the piano concerto is Mozart's most characteristic creation, this does not mean that he did not have any forerunners, or that he did not know them. The form was young, it is true. To its development, the Bach family, including the great father and two of his sons, the second and the youngest, had made the greatest contributions. About 1720 Johann Sebastian Bach adapted the Vivaldi concerto form to works for the clavier. This form consisted of three movements. We may say that it contained, typically, an *allegro maestoso,* an *andante* or *largo,* and a *presto.* The first movement imitated or expanded the form of the *prima parte* of a monumental aria—Aa—dD—a′A′; the capital letters indicate the tutti and the small letters the soli; A indicates the main stream of the thematic material, and D a sort of modulating thematic middle section that takes on more or less the character of a development. The second movement sometimes has the same form, but usually in more singing or melodic style—or, often, simply two-part song form. The third movement is usually a *rondeau,* and almost always of lower specific gravity than the first movement. Rarely does a concerto have so grand a conclusion as the glorious fugue in Johann Sebastian Bach's C major Concerto for two claviers, or in Philipp Emanuel's famous D minor Concerto of 1748. Now, it is certain that the young Mozart did not know any of Johann Sebastian's clavier concertos, and more than questionable whether he knew any of the forty-seven by Carl Philipp Emanuel. It is possible that in later years he made the acquaintance of the D minor Concerto just mentioned, of which the Finale has a strange but hardly tangible relation to the first movement of his own D minor Concerto. In van Swieten's library, Philipp Emanuel was certainly represented by some clavier concertos. But apart from the fact that Philipp Emanuel's spirit was not congenial to Mozart's, all his clavier concertos were intended specifically for the harpsichord—so completely so, in the nature of their invention and in their dynamics, that at the end of his life, in 1788, Philipp Emanuel could write a double concerto for harpsichord, piano, and orchestra. He was far too ingenious and vital a musician not to give the orchestra its own important role, along with the cembalo, and not to keep varying the concerto form. But Mozart was not influenced by him, or at least not directly so. The composer whose clavier concertos he came to know while still a child was a South-German, Georg Christoph Wagenseil, the old and highly respected teacher of the Hapsburg Archduchesses. His clavier works were shown to Mozart as early as 1764, in London, and a concerto by him for two claviers is expressly mentioned by Leopold as being in the family's possession (November 1767). Wagenseil, the South-German, was an agreeable musician who cultivated a much simpler form of the clavier concerto than Philipp Emanuel, of Berlin. But to Wagenseil's influence was very early added that of Johann Christian Bach. He it was who, in this domain as in so many others, for some time furnished Mozart's fantasy with its greatest stimulus. Or, if this statement seems too categorical, let us say that Mozart's fantasy took Bach's concerto form as its point of departure. For this statement we have documentary evidence. As a nine-year-old boy, in the summer or fall of 1765, Mozart converted three sonatas taken from Johann Christian's Op. V into concertos: *Tre Sonate del Sgr. Gio-*

vanni Bach ridotte in Concerti dal Sgr. Amadeo Wolfgango Mozart (K. 107). These works served Mozart as exercises in the concerto form, with Johann Christian's melodies as material. His procedure was extraordinarily primitive: he distributed the musical material between the two partners, shortening or lengthening the movements of each of the three works by alternating tutti and solo; the tutti consists simply of two violins and bass. But the three works were not intended to be exercises only; they were also to provide material for forthcoming tours. One could find two violins and a bass anywhere (even in the poorest court or the least musical town in Holland, France, or Switzerland) for an appearance by Wolfgang as soloist in a concerto, while most of the concertos of Johann Christian already available required an orchestra including two oboes and two horns. Mozart played the three works not just during his child-prodigy days, but also in later years, as is shown by two cadenzas for the first of the concertos, in D—cadenzas of which the handwriting and the style belong to a much later period. In 1767, in Salzburg, Mozart applied a similar procedure to a series of sonata-movements for the most part by "Parisian" composers—Hermann Fr. Raupach, Leontzi Honnauer—but also by Schobert, Eckard, and Philipp Emanuel Bach: a similar procedure, but not the same one, for now the solo part is a little more pretentious, and the tutti has the usual orchestration, with full strings, and the two pairs of wind instruments. The unity of style that prevailed in the *galant* period is so striking that until the work of discovery by Wyzewa and Saint-Foix it was possible to regard these four concertos (K. 37, 39, 40, 41) as "genuine Mozart."

It was at the end of 1773 that Mozart wrote his first really original clavier concerto, in D major (K. 175). In its instrumentation—which includes not only oboes and horns but trumpets and timpani as well—in its relation between soloist and orchestra, and in its length, it goes far beyond Johann Christian Bach, and one has the impression that Mozart knew this fact and wished to emphasize it. For in the development section, after only six measures of the solo part, the tutti enters with a so-called "false recapitulation"—a device Mozart does not usually greatly emphasize, and one that does not have at all the same significance in his works as in Haydn's. Now, Johann Christian would have begun the real recapitulation at this point, because in his concertos, intended as they were for the ornamentation of social functions, an elegant and ingratiating solo part was more important than any serious opposition between solo and tutti. Even in the Mozart work the recapitulation comes only twenty-two measures later, but during these twenty-two measures there are suggestions of perilous and somber regions, and it is by contrast with them that the royal majesty of the recapitulation is brought out. There is hardly a measure in the work in which there is not a lively relation in sound, and often a thematic relation as well, between the solo and the tutti, although the whole remains well within the bounds of *galanterie.* The same is true of the Andante (*ma un poco Adagio!*) in G major, a deeply felt movement despite all its *galanterie.* He writes a "learned," contrapuntal Finale, as in a few of the Vienna string quartets of 1773. But here he succeeds in something that was not quite successful in them. The canonic entrance of the theme in the tutti

is transformed in the following entrance of the solo part:

And this softened, *galant* version of the original "learned" and somewhat rigid material has been prepared by a subsidiary theme that would not be out of place even in the Finale of the "Jupiter" Symphony.

The wit and grace in the play of these two contrasting elements are inimitable; in this first attempt, Mozart has not only left Johann Christian and

Philipp Emanuel far behind, but has freed himself from them entirely. Did he later become dissatisfied with this movement, or was he no longer sure of its effect on the public? From Mannheim, he reports, diffidently (14 February 1778): "Then I played my old concerto in D major, because it is still a favorite here"; but for the public of Vienna he replaced the movement in 1782 with a set of Variations (K. 382)—Mozart himself called the new movement a "rondo"—which is a little miracle of humor when one considers all that is made of the alternation of tonics and dominants (and when one imagines how Mozart must have played it). But as a conclusion for this Concerto it does not maintain the style of the earlier movements. This is the first instance of Mozart's having to write down to the taste of the Vienna public.

For two years thereafter Mozart did not write any piano concertos. The interval, which lasted until January 1776, the date of the Concerto in B-flat (K. 238), was taken up with the composition of a concerto for bassoon, and five for violin. In the second Piano Concerto, more modest in its instrumentation than the first, we feel a certain reflection of the grace of the violin concertos and—in the Rondo, particularly—of the popular element in their finales:

although there are no real quotations, and no actual changes of meter as in the violin concertos. Mozart considered the piano concerto a higher species, and one of the finest and most expressive motives of the first movement of this Concerto recurred to him later, for Donna Elvira's entrance scene, in a more cajoling and seductive version:

The next Concerto, in C major (K. 246)—for we shall not concern ourselves further with the purely *galant* Concerto for Three Pianos—is almost a duplicate of its predecessor, except that the Andante is more pastoral and innocent in character, and the Rondo, a *Tempo di minuetto* with a piquant theme, withholds its trumps until after the cadenza. For this movement, incidentally, although not for the first and second movements, Mozart wrote out the cadenza in the score. The work was composed for Countess Antonia von Lützow, the second wife of the Commandant of the Veste Hohensalzburg, Johann Nepomuk Gottfried Count Lützow. The Countess was a pupil of Leopold's, and Mozart could write for her just as well as for himself, with little need of making concessions to her limitations. At any rate, he played the Concerto himself in Vienna, or wished to play it, for on 10 April 1782, he asked his father to send him the score.

In January 1777, the month in which Mozart celebrated his twenty-first birthday, he wrote a Concerto that is anything but a second replica of the first one (E-flat major, K. 271). He wanted to publish it together with the two preceding works in Paris (letter of 11 September 1778):

> As for my three concertos, the one written for Mlle. Jeunehomme, the one for Countess Lützow, and the one in B-flat, I shall sell them to the man who engraved my sonatas, provided he pays cash for them.

But the thought of paying cash never occurred to the engraver, Sieber, who was just as good a businessman as he was a musician; and for that fact no doubt this very Concerto for Mlle. Jeunehomme (or "Jenomy," as Mozart called her) was to blame. Customers who might have liked the two previous concertos would certainly have rejected this one. It is surprising and unique among Mozart's works. Nothing in the products of the year 1776 leads us to expect it, for the Divertimento K. 247, although it is a masterpiece in its own field, is nothing more than a joyous *Final-Musik.* This concerto, on the other hand, is one of Mozart's monumental works, those works in which he is entirely himself, seeking not to ingratiate himself with his public but rather to win them through originality and boldness. He never surpassed it. There are similar bold ventures, full of both youth and maturity, in the works of other great masters: the wedding panel by Titian known as "Sacred and Profane Love," Goethe's *Werther,* Beethoven's *Eroica.* This E-flat major Concerto is Mozart's "Eroica." It embodies not only a profound contrast, and accordingly a higher unity, among its three movements, but also the most intimate relation of soloist and orchestra; and the orchestra itself is treated with greater vitality and more finely wrought detail than before, in truly symphonic style. The middle movement, an Andantino, is a striking example. It is in C minor, the first minor movement in a Mozart concerto, and thus a forerunner of the C minor Andante of the *Sinfonia Concertante* of 1779, for violin and viola. The strings are muted, with a canon between Violins I and II. The solo does not repeat the tutti, but rather comments upon it in free singing style. The melody of the whole movement is so eloquent that at any moment it could break into genuine recitative. In the last measures, the mutes disappear, and restraint is cast off in favor of actual recitative. The first and last movements are fitting companions to this slow movement. In the building up of the very first theme, the orchestra and the soloist collaborate. The soloist is in command, in full and proud sovereignty, but, for the first time, he permits himself to accompany a member of the orchestra, the first oboe, in simple chords. What a contrast with the concertos of Johann Christian, in which the solo part does sometimes feature simple chords, while in the orchestra—nothing happens; for in these works the concerto ideal never goes beyond the conception of a solo with accompaniment. The inner agitation responsible for the creation of this concerto brought about a constant succession of surprises, both in the structure and in the smallest details; nothing is left, not even the cadenzas, to chance or routine. The greatest surprise is the interpolation of a real minuet, in A-flat, with four variations, in the midst of the brilliant virtuosity of the *presto Finale.* But this is no excursion into the field of the popular, as in the violin concertos. This minuet is serious, elegant, stately, and expressive, all at once; it reflects the deep agitation of the Andantino, which is still seeking appeasement. There is nowhere any straining for virtuosity; yet this Concerto makes higher demands, technically as well as otherwise, than its predecessors. One would like to know something more about Mlle. Jeunehomme, who inspired Mozart to write such a work, but for the present she remains a legendary figure.

In Paris [1] Mozart felt no urge to write a new piano concerto, and for Mannheim, too, both before the visit to Paris and afterwards, the compositions he already had sufficed. But his work on the *Sinfonia Concertante,* the big work for the four wind-instrument players of Mannheim; the concerto for flute and harp written for the Duc de Guines and his daughter; the ambitious project of a double concerto for clavier and violin—all this bore fruit. After his return home, Mozart wrote the Concerto for Two Pianos in E-flat major, for himself and Nannerl (K. 365). It is a companion piece both to the *Sinfonia Concertante* in the same key (K. 364), which it cannot quite equal, and to the Vienna Sonata for Two Pianos, in D major (K. 448, written in 1781), which is likewise not to be matched. But the Concerto contains a brilliant contest between the two players, and the orchestra, with its majestic beginning, enters significantly into this eager dialogue—unforgettably, above all, in a horn call in the cadence of a subsidiary theme.

But there is not only a brilliant contest. Side by side with places of what one might call 'mechanical' gaiety, as for example the following:

1. Einstein is referring to Mozart's important trip to Paris, by way of Mannheim, in 1777–78. [*Editor*]

there is a strange darkening of the mood in the recapitulation. The pastoral Andante, too, quivers with a mood of longing, and has passages of extraordinary luxuriance. And even in the Rondo, which is frankly merry, the middle portion, in C minor, moves into what seem dangerous and mysterious regions—regions, too, of contrapuntal seriousness. But the seriousness is not quite so deep as might appear, as is shown by the fact that Mozart later borrowed one of the C minor passages and put it into the mouth of Papageno, just at the point where the latter's comic anxiety reaches its peak. In general, the Concerto is a work of happiness, gaiety, overflowing richness of invention, and joy in itself, and thus is evidence of how little the secret of creative activity has to do with personal experience, for it was written just after the bitterest disappointments of Mozart's life.[2] In the early years in Vienna he performed it several times with Fräulein Aurnhammer, and for these occasions he enriched the instrumentation of the opening and closing movements by the addition of clarinets, trumpets and timpani. We know the work only in its more modest Salzburg garb, in which the orchestra takes a really active part only in the Rondo.

It seems to me that in this simpler concerto, or rather in the simpler relation of the solo part to the orchestra in it, there are reflections of a musical acquaintance Mozart had made in the summer of 1778, in Paris: the Six Clavier Concertos, Op. III, by Johann Samuel Schröter. "Write and tell me whether you have Schröter's concertos in Salzburg—and Hüllmandel's sonatas. If not, I should like to buy them and send them to you. Both works are very fine." Such an estimate by Mozart must be taken seriously. Who was Johann Samuel Schröter? He was the son of a Saxon musician, an oboist in Warsaw, who in 1763 had been seeking a place in his native Saxony for his family of four children. For his daughter Corona, then a girl of twelve, he found a place promptly; Corona Schröter, who later in Weimar set Goethe's heart aflame (among others), needs no further introduction. Johann Samuel, who was probably a little older than his sister Corona, became a clavier virtuoso, and in 1772 went to London, where he made his debut in the Bach-Abel concerts, just as Mozart, six or seven years earlier, had been taken under Johann Christian's wing. In 1782, he became Johann Christian's successor as music master to the Queen, and like Mozart he died young, on 2 November 1788. He retired quite early from public life, that being the condition of his marriage with

2. His rejection by Aloysia Weber, a singer with whom he had fallen in love. He later married her sister Constanze. [*Editor*]

a pupil, a rich girl from a high-born family. The lady in question later played a romantic role in the life of Joseph Haydn, on the occasion of his first visit to London: she took lessons of Haydn and fell in love with the youthful old man, and Haydn does not seem to have been indifferent to her charms—at least he conscientiously copied out all her love letters.

Now Mozart certainly could not learn anything technically from Schröter. These concertos, Op. III, which are soli with a sparse accompaniment of two violins and bass, are very simple in structure, quite in the style of the concertos of Johann Christian, but even lighter and more primitive. They have, however, the greatest melodic charm and innocence. At times they seem to speak with the voice of Mozart himself, and it seems to me that between the Larghetto of Schröter's Op. III, No. 6,

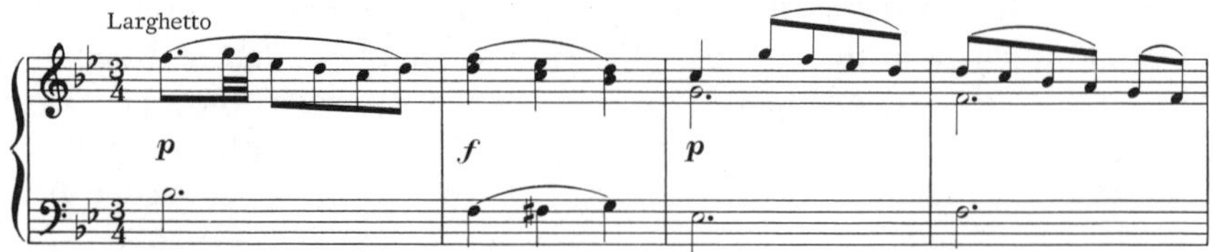

and the Andante in the Double Concerto of which we have been speaking,

there is a direct connection. For three of the concertos of Schröter Mozart wrote cadenzas, which is proof that he either played them himself or had his pupils play them.

There is another feature for which Mozart seems to have found the inspiration in Schröter's Op. III—a most characteristic feature. Schröter wrote his clavier concertos for his own performance, but also for amateur performers among the ladies of London, and accordingly he did not bother with any development section in the first movement, or with any organic relation between the solo and the tutti. For this, he substituted a free solo, thematically unrelated to the rest of the movement, which led back to the recapitulation, and was often of great and even enchanting beauty. This made a deep impression on Mozart, who imitated it—not, to be sure, in the first movements of his piano quartets, piano trios, or piano concertos, in which so great and serious a master as he could not renounce development, but in the finales. There have been and will be many occasions, in the course of this book, to speak of the great artistic wisdom and sense of effect displayed by Mozart in such instances.

It seems as if Mozart still had in mind the ideal of the amiable clavier concertos of Schröter when, in the fall of 1782 and the first months of 1783, he wrote his first three Vienna works in this form. Or perhaps it was that he knew his public, and wished to charm them with amiability rather than risk offending them by too aggressive originality. From the very first he was thinking of publication—publication in Paris, where he had made the acquaintance of the Schröter concertos, and where he felt he could hope for a particularly good reception. At first, in January 1783, he offered them in Vienna in manuscript copies at a subscription price of 4 ducats; but as early as 26 April he wrote to the Parisian publisher, J. G. Sieber:

> . . . I have three piano concertos ready, which can be performed with full orchestra, that is to say with oboes and horns, or merely a quattro. Artaria wants to engrave them. But I give you, my friend, the first refusal . . .

However, Sieber either replied that he did not wish to pay the thirty louis d'or that Mozart demanded or else did not reply at all, for the three concertos were published by Artaria in Vienna two years later, in March 1785, as Op. IV.

The alternative possibilities provided for by Mozart in these concertos—performance either by full orchestra including oboes and horns (in the third one, in C major, including trumpets and timpani also), or by string quartet—are enough to show that we are not dealing with "great" concertos. The winds are not essential, as they contribute nothing not fully expressed by the strings; their function is only to lend color or rhythmic emphasis. These works may very well be played as chamber music by a pianist with string quartet accompaniment. No one characterized them better than Mozart himself (letter of 28 December 1782 ["These concertos are a happy medium between what is too easy and too difficult; they are very brilliant, pleasing to the ear, and natural, without being vapid. There are passages here and there from which connoisseurs alone can derive satisfaction; but these passages are written in such a way that the less learned cannot fail to be pleased, though without knowing why . . ."]). How naïve and at the same time how penetrating are his esthetics! And what a high moral standard underlies them: the composer must make things hard for himself and easy for the listener. The fact that Mozart did indeed make things hard for himself is shown by the existence of a second Rondo (K. 386) for the first of the three Concertos (in A major, K. 414), which he left in the form of a sketch so complete that there is no difficulty about supplying the little that is missing. No doubt the reason for abandoning it was that it repeated certain melodic turns of phrase that had appeared in the first movement. To us it seems at least as attractive as the Rondo Mozart used for this work, and perhaps even superior to it. The warmest and most alive movement of this charming little Concerto is the Andante, with its Schubertean *appoggiature* in the cadence:

and with its romantic, murmuring accompaniment figure in thirds. One has the impression that this movement must have been composed after the Concerto in F (K. 413), which breathes nothing but amiability throughout its three movements, and offers something special to "connoisseurs" only in the fine contrapuntal writing of the Rondo, a *Tempo di minuetto*; perhaps also in the triple meter of the first movement, triple meter being very unusual in a first movement. Mozart obviously wished to offer three very different types of concertos, contrasting in key, and each typical in its own key. If the first is rather naïve and pastoral, and the second more poetic and *amoureux,* the last, in C major, with its trumpets and timpani, is the most brilliant and the most conventional, but it, too, is full of individual details and refinements. Mozart originally wished to write the second movement in C minor, but soon realized that that would make it much too serious for the character of these works, and instead wrote one of the least ambitious slow movements in any of his works. To make up for this, he inserted in the Finale, in which we already hear some of Papageno's $\frac{6}{8}$ motives, a C minor episode, which, in these surroundings, and with exaggerated ornamentation, is almost comically doleful. The principle of surprise is carried so far in this Finale as to make it almost a *capriccio.*

At any rate, Mozart succeeded in pleasing the taste of the Viennese. We read in a report in *Cramer's Magazin* for 22 March 1783 (I, 578):

> Today the celebrated Chevalier Mozart gave a music academy for his own benefit at the National-Theater in which pieces of his own composition, which was already very popular, were performed. The academy was honored by the presence of an extraordinarily large audience and the *two new concertos* and other fantasies which Mr. Mozart played on the Forte Piano were received with the loudest approval. Our Monarch, who contrary to his custom honored the whole academy with his presence, joined in the applause of the public so heartily that one can think of no similar example. The proceeds of the academy are estimated at sixteen hundred gulden.

We do not know which two of the three Concertos Mozart played.

On 9 February 1784, Mozart began to enter in a little notebook of forty-four leaves—perhaps a bit too large to have served as a pocket notebook—all his works as he completed them, giving in each case the date, the type, and the beginning of the work written on two staves. He kept up this book until a few weeks before his death, filling fifty-eight pages. The first work he listed is a Concerto for piano in E-flat major (K. 449), with accompaniment for strings, and oboes and horns *ad libitum*. The fact that the participation of the winds is made optional seems to connect this Concerto with the three written in 1782-3; but the connection is only apparent. Mozart dedicated the work to his pupil Barbara Ployer, the daughter of a fellow-native of Salzburg then living in Vienna, and evidently did not wish to deprive her of the possibility of playing it with a small combination of instruments in a drawing-room. Actually, however, the wind instruments, although they seem sparingly used, can hardly be omitted; and this Concerto is not really a continuation of the type of the Salzburg concertos and the first three composed in Vienna, but a new beginning—the beginning of a new series comprising no less than twelve great concertos, written between 9 February 1784 and 4 December 1786, and constituting the high-point of Mozart's instrumental composition. This series is followed by only the Coronation Concerto in D major and the last one, in B-flat major, written in January of the year of Mozart's death.

Immediately after the concerto for Fräulein Ployer, he composed two more, in B-flat (K. 450) and in D (K. 451), and then, after the Piano Quintet (K. 452), still another, in G major (K. 453), a miracle of productivity in no way less extraordinary than the miracle of the three symphonies of 1788.[3] For all these works are as different from one another as can be imagined. In an illuminating passage in a letter to his father, dated 26 May 1784, Mozart expressed himself briefly about them. He mentioned the two concertos in B-flat and D, and continued:

> I really cannot choose between the two of them, but I regard them both as concertos that are bound to make the performer sweat. From the point of view of difficulty the B♭ concerto beats the one in D. Well, I am very curious to hear which of the three, in B♭, D, and G, you and my sister prefer. The one in E♭ does not belong at all to the same category. It is one of a quite peculiar kind, composed rather for a small orchestra than for a large one . . .

The E-flat Concerto is indeed "of a quite peculiar kind." Mozart never wrote another like it, either before or afterwards. Yet, there is a connection between the Finale of this work and the original Finale of Mozart's first Concerto (K. 175). Mozart had in the meantime experienced his contrapuntal crisis,[4] and he wrote a Finale that is full of the contrapuntal spirit:

But what eleven or twelve years earlier had been in some degree contrapuntal display had now become the free play of Mozart's creative gift, his natural idiom, the expression of the most complete mastery, a miracle of the fusion of styles. This work has a thematic variety and unity and an ingenuity of form that reveal the joy of the creative spirit at its highest. The first movement, too, is somewhat exceptional among Mozart's works. It voices an unrest that never tires of inventing contrasting themes. This movement, like the first movement of K. 413, is in $\frac{3}{4}$ time, and one is tempted to say that it seeks to express in E-flat major what a later movement in the same meter completely realizes—the one in the C minor Piano Concerto, K. 491. The element of unrest intensifies an old tendency in Mozart's language: a leaning towards the use of the chromatic, in both melody and harmony. A deep inner experience, about the exact nature

3. The Symphonies in E-flat, G minor, and C ("Jupiter"), written within a space of three months during 1788. [*Editor*]

4. Einstein refers to Mozart's exposure in the early Vienna years to the music of J. S. Bach, which had a deep influence on his musical style. [*Editor*]

of which we know nothing, is revealed in the more rapid changes of dynamics, the more refined and at the same time bolder chromaticism, the unity of the motives, demonstrable though concealed—in short, in a new degree of sensitiveness. At the same time, and particularly in the slow movement, an Andantino, Mozart seems to have grown simpler, and to be more than ever avoiding pathos and sentimentality. It is characteristic that in a letter to his father he emphasized the fact that none of these concertos has an Adagio. The superficial listener is to have his pleasure in them without noticing the deeper things they contain.

In the next two works, which are twins, in B-flat (K. 450) and D (K. 451), Mozart returns to more familiar paths. He uses a large orchestra, including in K. 451 trumpets and timpani, and in the Finale of K. 450, for the first time in a finale, the flute. The winds are essential, both as soloists and as a body. The orchestra is treated symphonically, with dialogue among its own members, and this leads naturally to a more brilliant treatment of the piano part. One hardly knows whether to call these works, particularly the second, piano concertos with obbligato orchestra or symphonies with obbligato piano solo.[5] Both works are in the highest degree brilliant and personal. Mozart wishes to conquer his public, but without sacrificing anything of his own individuality. The B-flat major Concerto seems quite regular. Even the free fantasy *in tempo*—Mozart calls such a passage *Eingang* (entrance)—which precedes the entry of the theme in the solo part in the first movement, is not an unusual feature. The second movement consists of simple variations on a simple melody, with the repetitions distributed between the soloist and the orchestra, and a free conclusion. The Finale is a hunting scene. The D major Concerto seems like nothing more than a heroic and exuberant quick-march, with a song-like Andante, and a Rondo *à la* Joseph Haydn. Everything seems familiar and popular; yet at every instant there are surprises, an exuberance of spirit and a feeling of power, and unexpected refinements—like the *piano* passage in the recapitulation of the triumphal and yet passionate first movement, or the contrapuntal climax at the end of the second, or the very serious development section in the Rondo. The nineteenth century gradually lost any understanding for such things, since it had lost the feeling for any definite framework, or any given forms. But Mozart's public included some listeners who could appreciate every subtle divergence from the expected. That is the special quality of these Concertos—

5. The second of these alternatives would have been resisted by Tovey, who was at pains to draw a distinction between concerto and symphony style (see below). [*Editor*]

the fact that, in Mozart's own phrase, they are "written for all kinds of ears, not just for the long ones." Incidentally we may observe that few listeners had better musical ears than Mozart's sister Marianne. She pointed out a passage in the Andante in the D major Concerto that was too bare, and Mozart agreed with her and promised in a letter of 9–12 June 1784 to send her an ornamented variant. This variant survives, and is evidence that Mozart did not always play the solo part in the form in which it has come down to us. We shall return to this problem in connection with the second Coronation Concerto.

Mozart crowned the series of piano concertos written in this astonishing winter of 1784 with one in G major (K. 453), again intended *per la Signora Barbara Ployer,* as the inscription on the autograph tells us. On 10 June there was an "academy" in the country, at Ployer's house in Döbling—"a concert, where Fräulein Babette is playing her new concerto in G, and I am performing the quintet [K. 452], we are then playing together the grand sonata for two claviers." This concerto, too, is unique. It is more intimate than its three predecessors; it welds the solo and orchestra parts into a closer unity, its friendly key is full of hidden laughter and hidden sadness. No words can describe the continuous iridescence of feeling of the first movement, or the passionate tenderness of the second. The fact that this C major movement goes as far afield as G-sharp major is only an external sign of its passionate quality. The Finale consists of variations on a naïve, birdlike, Papageno sort of theme with a grandiose, polyphonic conclusion. Mr. Girdlestone has rightly remarked that Beethoven's most amiable concerto, in the same key, takes its departure from this work of Mozart's. But the concerto of Beethoven, who could not be naïve, is powerful and robust in comparison with the delicate shadings of this unique work, which has no parallel even among Mozart's other compositions.

The year 1784 brought forth two more concertos still, very different from the preceding ones and from each other. The first, again in B-flat (K. 456), which Mozart completed after recovering from a very heavy cold caught at the première of *Il Re Teodoro* by Casti and Paisiello, is distinguished by the fact that he wrote it neither for himself nor for a pupil as talented and close to him as Babette Ployer (for himself or for Babette he would certainly not have chosen B-flat again) but for another Vienna virtuoso, Maria Theresa Paradis. This young lady, who had been blind since childhood, and was at that time twenty-five years old. was the daughter of a State Councilor of Lower Austria, and a godchild of the Empress. She was a pupil of Leopold Kozeluch, and she could play, according to Gerber, "more than sixty clavier concertos [by Kozeluch] with the greatest accuracy and the finest expression, in every way worthy of her teacher." It is evidence of Mozart's broadmindedness, or of his indifference, that he wrote a new concerto for the pupil of his deadly enemy to perform in Paris, whither a concert tour brought her in the autumn of 1784. For Paris, obviously, Kozeluch's concertos did not suffice. Kozeluch was, again quoting Gerber:

> without doubt, among young and old, the most generally popular of all composers now living, and that quite rightly. His works are characterized by cheerfulness and grace, the noblest melody combined with the purest harmony and the most pleasing arrangement in respect to rhythm and modulation.

Now Mozart gave even the Parisians, whom he so hated, credit for desiring something more than that. So he harked back a little to Schobert, Johann Christian Bach, and Schröter. The relations of the solo part and the orchestra in this work are, to be sure, purely Mozartean, characteristic only of him, and perhaps even closer than ever before; but the solo part has a different, more "feminine," more sensuous character than the preceding concertos, and that iridescence of expression characteristic of the second Ployer Concerto is almost completely absent. In the Ployer Concerto there is nothing like the modulation to B minor in this Parisian one, emphasized as it is by the combination of $\frac{6}{8}$ and $\frac{2}{4}$ meters. But Schröter, too, had indulged in such pseudodrama, and the Parisians were fond of that sort of thing. The slow movement consists of variations with coda, in G minor. Their tearful character already has something to do with the loss of Barbarina's pin in *Figaro*; it is very French. The work is full of miracles of sonority, but it contains none of the "surprises," great or small, of the great concertos.

The last concerto of 1784, the one in F major (K. 459), finished on 11 December, was surely written with Mozart himself alone in mind. This work exhibits a fine sense of climax. Each of the three movements is more beautiful than the preceding, so that one might almost call it a finale-concerto. The first movement, with its persistent march rhythm, shows more strongly than any other concerto of Mozart's the influence of the violin concertos of Viotti. We know that Mozart composed a new middle movement for Viotti's 16th Concerto, and this can hardly have been his first acquaintance with the works of the great violinist of Piedmont, who, as Gerber says, had been "famous since 1783," and had already toured the entire continent. Now the "ideal march" is typical of Viotti's first movements; there is hardly one among his twenty-nine concertos that does not have all the characteristics of such an ideal march—the firm step, the dotted rhythms, the military bearing. The seriousness of many of these concertos, too, must have made an impression on Mozart. One of the earlier ones, the 6th, issued in 1782 or 1783, is in D minor. Now the military element had not been foreign to Mozart's concertos even before this, but he had never emphasized it as strongly as in this movement, in which such motives as:

are almost everywhere present. Joyful assurance—that is the character of this movement. At the same time, it seems in a way like a festal introduction to the Allegretto in C—not, be it noted, in B-flat—which, in its charming and so often melancholy dreaming, is like an instrumental version, or a projection into the infinite realm of the instrumental, of all the emotions that are later expressed in Susanna's aria *Deh vieni, non tardar*. The last movement exhibits the play of all the spirits of Ariel's troupe, with Colombina, Arlecchino, and Papageno joining them now and again. This is *opera buffa* translated into the domain of instrumental music, and at the same time a masterful play with the 'learned' element, a fusion of homophony and polyphony—one of the few instances in which Mozart uses counterpoint in mocking vein. This Finale contains a few rhythms that are to be found note for note in Mozart's pantomime for the Carnival of 1783 (K. 446).

It is strange to think that Brahms once thought of Viotti's concertos in connection with Mozart's: "The fact that people in general *do not* understand and *do not* respect the very best things, such as Mozart's concertos and the A minor Concerto by Viotti—that is what permits men like us to live and become famous." We may hope that Wagner was not thinking of this piece, among others, when he distinguished the "absolute allegro" from the "characteristic Beethoven allegro":

> What further stamps the Mozartean *absolute Allegro* as specifically belonging to the naïve order, is its simple play of *forte* and *piano,* on the side of dynamics, as also, in respect of formal structure, its random juxtaposition [*wahllose Nebeneinanderstellung*] of certain stock melodic-

> rhythmic forms adapted to the *piano* or the *forte* method, in whose employment (as in the perpetual repetition of the selfsame thunderous half-closes) the master shows an almost more than startling [*eine fast mehr als überraschende*] unconstraint. Yet everything here, even the most heedless use of altogether banal phrases, explains itself by just the character of this Allegro: it has no desire to chain us by a cantilena, but to plunge us into a certain tumult through its restless motion . . .[6]

Poor "master"! It is evident that Wagner's "penetrating" description applies more to Mozart's overtures, but that is not important. For it is not really accurate as applied to the overtures either. One might say on the contrary that no master made less use of formulas than Mozart, and that none did more to transform formulas into expressive material, though not, of course, expressive in the sense of nineteenth-century Romanticism.

On the occasion of the coronation of Leopold II, on 15 October 1790, in Frankfurt-am-Main, Mozart played this Concerto together with the so-called Coronation Concerto (K. 537), with trumpets and timpani in the tutti. The latter were not added for the occasion, but belonged originally to the score. The parts are lost, but they should be prudently restored to the first and last movements: the first movement unquestionably needs them for its "military" brilliance, and the humor of the Finale would gain here and there in effectiveness.

There could be no greater contrast than exists between this work and the one following, dated 10 February 1785, barely eight or nine weeks later. This is the D minor Concerto, K. 466, Mozart's first piano concerto in the minor mode, and the one best known, one might almost say the only one known, in the nineteenth century. That fact reveals a great deal about the nineteenth century, which did not understand the sublime humor of the F major Concerto, but well understood what distinguished the D minor among all the piano concertos of Mozart: passion, pathos, drama. This Concerto made it possible to stamp Mozart as a forerunner of Beethoven, and it is indeed no accident that for this very Concerto Beethoven wrote cadenzas—a splendid one, fusing the Mozart and Beethoven styles, for the first movement, and a rather weaker one for the last. This is the first work in which the tutti and the solo in the Allegro are sharply contrasted, in a dualism there is no attempt to overcome. The orchestra represents an anonymous threatening power, and the solo instrument voices an eloquent lament. The orchestra never takes over the

6. *About Conducting,* translated by William Ashton Ellis, IV, 318.

first theme of the solo part, a *recitativo in tempo,* or the second half of the second theme. The opposition of the two permits of no reconciliation; it is only intensified in the development section. Nor does the reprise offer any solution: the *pianissimo* conclusion of the movement is as if the furies had simply become tired out and had lain down to rest, still grumbling, and ready at any instant to take up the fight again. And they do take it up again, in the middle section (in G minor) of the *Romanza,* which begins and ends in such heavenly tranquillity. Mozart never included stronger contrasts within a single work, contrasts among the three movements as well as within each movement individually. The choice of key for the Andante is revealing: not F major, or D major, but the subdominant of the relative major, just as in the G minor Symphony three years later. The Finale contains chromatically intensified and refined passion and drama, announced at the very beginning in the rocket-like principal motive. But this time Mozart wishes to conquer his pessimism and despair. After the cadenza, he turns towards the major, in a coda of enchanting sweetness, which represents at the same time an affecting ray of light and, in slight degree, a return to the social atmosphere of earlier works, the courtly gesture of a grand seigneur who wishes to leave his guests with a friendly impression. But this is not at all the childlike or grandiose optimism of Haydn or Beethoven.

One cannot say that in the Concerto immediately following this passionate work, the one in C major, K. 467, dated 9 March 1785, Mozart returned to "normality": normality and classicism in the usual sense are terms that can hardly be applied to Mozart's music, above all in the Vienna period. But what Mozart does return to is the proud, triumphant affirmation of himself, once again symbolized by an ideal march, of which the theme begins:

This motive waits throughout the entire movement to establish itself. It is symbolized in the fanfares of the winds and in a subsidiary theme of that utmost simplicity of which only great men are capable, men who possess that "second naïveté," which is the highest achievement of artistic and human experience. And Mozart returns from dramatic dialogue to symphonic treatment. Up to this time he had written no more imposing counter-melodies than the one in measures 13–20 of the tutti. The passage must be quoted complete and in its full scoring to make its significance clear:

The whole Concerto, but particularly the development, with its modulations through darkness into light, is one of the most beautiful examples of Mozart's iridescent harmony and of the breadth of the domain embraced in his conception of the key of C major. The Finale, which is a *buffo finale* again, is built up entirely on harmony enlivened with chromaticism, and on gay motives entirely lacking, this time, in any "learned" quality. The Andante, with its muted strings, its quivering triplets, its *pizzicato* accompaniment against the broad arch of the soloist's cantilena, is like an ideal aria freed of all the limitations of the human voice. When one listens to such a work, one understands why Mozart wrote no symphonies in the earlier Vienna years, for these concertos are symphonic in the highest sense, and Mozart did not need to turn to the field of the pure symphony until that of the concerto was closed to him.

During the period of his work on *Le Nozze di Figaro,* in the winter and during the Carnival time of 1785–6, Mozart again completed three piano concertos: in E-flat (K. 482), in A (K. 488), and in C minor (K. 491). The first two give us the impression that he felt he had perhaps gone too far, had given the Viennese public credit for too much, had overstepped the boundaries of "social" music—or, more simply stated, that he saw the favor of the public waning, and sought to win it back with works that would be sure of success. The first, especially, is a return—a return to the sphere of the earlier E-flat Concertos, the Concerto for Two Claviers and K. 271. The connection is palpable—externally visible, even: in the Allegro, in the motives of the horns (the winds, among which for the first time clarinets replace the oboes, play an enhanced role in this work altogether) or in the Finale, a "hunting" movement transfigured into a round-dance, in the minuet-like episode in A-flat which looks backward to the finale of K. 271 and forward to the canon in the second Finale of *Così fan tutte.* Everything reveals a certain routine, not of craftsmanship but of the spirit. But this is true only of the first and last movements. The slow movement, an Andante in C minor, a combination of song and variations, introduces a powerful element: expression unadorned, almost an exhibition of sadness, false consolation, despair, and resignation. Mozart exploits the contrast of major and minor in an entirely new way—that of the nineteenth century. It is significant of the cultural state of Vienna at the time that the public, at a subscription concert of Mozart's on 23 December, understood the direct appeal of the movement and demanded its repetition. Mozart himself was astonished. Leopold wrote to his daughter, on 13 January 1786, that Wolfgang had written him two weeks previously that he had "composed . . . a new piano concerto in E♭, in which (a rather unusual occurrence!) he had to repeat the Andante."

In the A major Concerto Mozart again succeeded in meeting his public half-way without sacrificing anything of his own individuality. He never wrote another first movement so simple in its structure, so "normal" in its thematic relations between tutti and solo, or so clear in its thematic invention, even where it makes excursions into the realm of counterpoint, or contains rhythmic peculiarities. The key of A major is for Mozart the key of many colors. It has the transparency of a stained-glass window. There are relations between the first movement of this Concerto and the Clarinet Quintet. Not without reason are there no trumpets and timpani. But there are also darker shadings and concealed intensities, which the listener interested only in pleasant entertainment misses altogether. Already in this movement there is a threatening touch of F-sharp minor, and the whole Andante is in that key, which Mozart otherwise avoided. The latter movement is short, but it contains the soul of the work. It is the minor counterpart of the Andante of the "Prague" Symphony, even in the way it dissolves all polyphonic elements in a new style. In this movement there appears in veiled form that passion which in the Andante of the preceding Concerto had revealed itself nakedly; the resignation and the hopelessness are the same. And when Mozart overcomes this impression with the entrance of the rondo theme, he is a true magician. This Presto seems to introduce a breath of fresh air and a ray of sunlight into a dark and musty room. The gaiety of this uninterrupted stream of melody and rhythm is irresistible. But this is no ordinary gaiety. Again, as in the E-flat major Piano Quartet, or the B-flat major Piano Trio, the clarinet introduces one of those "unrelated" themes (in D major) in which the world seems perfectly balanced, and the scheme of things is fully justified. The work reverses the course of another work in A major, the Violin Sonata K. 526, in which the Andante is the movement of tranquillity, and the Finale sets loose a whole world of demons —another evidence of the breadth of Mozart's conception of the individuality of keys.

The passion that is veiled in the Andante of the A major Concerto breaks out again vehemently in the Concerto in C minor, finished on 24 March 1786, which bears the Köchel number immediately preceding that of *Figaro*. It seems as if Mozart wished to exhaust the key that he had previously, in the Andante of the E-flat major Concerto, used for an effect not quite legitimate, according to his conception of art as a heightened expression of feeling. At the same time there is a secret connection between this great, somber work and the C minor Serenade for Wind Instruments, of 1782. The Concerto is related to *Figaro* as the Serenade is to *Die Entführung,* even though the Serenade was not finished until shortly after the completion of the *Singspiel.* But in March 1786 *Figaro* was also practically finished. In both instances, Mozart evidently needed to indulge in an explosion of the dark, tragic, passionate emotions. There is a connection of a different sort with the Clavier Concerto in D minor, which shows Mozart's concerto form at its most dramatic. This C minor Concerto is another one that is a little Beethovenish; at least Beethoven admired it, and paid a certain homage to it in his own C minor Concerto, Op. 37. But Mozart's C minor Concerto is superior to the one in D minor. It is symphonic rather than simply in dialogue form, and the use of the richest orchestration Mozart had ever employed in a concerto—including both oboes and clarinets and with the wind instruments, both soli and as a body, taking a more prominent part than ever—is only external evidence of this fact. The passion in this work is deeper. Its affirmations of the key—all the modulations, no matter how far they wander, seem only to confirm the principal key—are more inevitable, more inexorable. Even when E-flat major is arrived at, the way remains strait and thorny.

Nothing is left of the ideal march; this first movement is in $\frac{3}{4}$ meter. Nothing is left of any compromise with social music, as in the Finale of the D minor Concerto; this Finale is an uncanny, revolutionary quick-march consisting of variations with free "episodes" (actually anything but episodes), which represent glimpses of Elysian fields—but the conclusion is a return to the inevitable.

It is hard to imagine the expression on the faces of the Viennese public when on 7 April 1786 Mozart played this work at one of his subscription concerts. Perhaps they contented themselves with the Larghetto, which moves in regions of the purest and most moving tranquillity, and has a transcendent simplicity of expression.

Mozart closed his great period of concerto writing with a concerto in C major, K. 503, finished on 4 December 1786. He followed it directly with the "Prague" Symphony—the first of a new and illustrious though brief series—and a few months later turned to a new species, in the C major Quintet, which may be said to have usurped the place of the concerto. For the piano concertos that were still to come are minor works and not the product of the primary creative urge that had brought forth the great concertos. But the C major Concerto is a grandiose conclusion. It is related both to the C major Concerto, K. 467, and to its immediate predecessor, in C minor: it is an intensification of K. 467, mightier and more exalted, and is a necessary self-affirmation after the desperate passion of the C minor Concerto. In it, victory is attained, symbolized most simply and indisputably in the triumphal march-theme of the first movement, which, significantly, first enters in minor, and needs no *forte:*

The battle is won. Whatever shadows the work contains are reminiscent only, even in the most passionate and agitated episode of the Rondo, which is not a humorous movement but a serious and self-confident one. No other work of Mozart's has such dimensions, and the dimensions correspond to the power of the symphonic construction and the drastic nature of the modulations. In no other concerto does the relation between the soloist and the orchestra vary so constantly and so unpredictably. The Adagio—for it is an adagio, and not at all, despite the marking, an andante [7]—is to be compared perhaps only to the C major Symphony for its lofty singing character and fullness, and for the vitality of its detail. True, the nobility of the conception is not always quite matched in the execution. At times one has the impression that Mozart was in a hurry, and Mr. Girdlestone rightly points out the comparative indifference displayed by Mozart at the conclusion of the Rondo, a point in the structure at which he usually played his highest trump. But what does

7. Girdlestone makes the same point: see p. 166. [*Editor*]

that matter when we consider the climaxes of this work in which the concentration of the themes is pushed to the utmost, without any impairment of the forward-driving *élan* of the whole?

To the penultimate concerto, written fourteen months later (24 February 1788; K. 537), in D major, we may quite properly apply the term *hors d'œuvre*. This work is known as the Coronation Concerto, because Mozart played it, along with K. 459, on 15 October 1790 in Frankfurt, during the festivities attending the coronation of Leopold II; and probably, even on that occasion, it had a greater success than the other work, which is much finer, more individual, and more ambitious. It was written for the concerts of Lent, 1788. We do not know whether Mozart ever played it in Vienna, but he took it with him on his trip to Berlin, and played it at Court in Dresden in April 1789. Nor can it be determined whether it was for this occasion or for Frankfurt that he added the trumpets and timpani to the score. But there is no question that it was the proper work for festive occasions. It is very Mozartean, while at the same time it does not express the whole or even the half of Mozart. It is, in fact, so "Mozartesque" that one might say that in it Mozart imitated himself —no difficult task for him. It is both brilliant and amiable, especially in the slow movement; it is very simple, even primitive, in its relation between the solo and the tutti, and so completely easy to understand that even the nineteenth century always grasped it without difficulty. It has become, along with the D minor, the best known of Mozart's piano concertos. This popularity illustrates once again the strange fact that those works are often held to be particularly characteristic which do not survive in wholly authentic form. For Mozart left the solo part of this concerto in an especially sketchy state. Now, we do not know exactly how he played any of his concertos. Only four were published during his lifetime, and while in his autographs he wrote out the orchestra parts with complete care, he did not do the same with the solo parts; indeed it would have been in his interest not to write them out at all, so as not to lead unscrupulous copyists into temptation. For he knew perfectly well what he had to play. The solo parts in the form in which they survive are always only a suggestion of the actual performance, and a constant invitation to read the breath of life into them. But the solo part of this D major Concerto in particular is no more than a bare sketch, obviously entered into the score by Mozart simply to refresh his memory, consisting mostly of a single line with only the more polyphonic passages written out for both hands. Suffice it to say that only the accompaniment of the rondo theme survives in Mozart's own authentic version. Who was responsible for the version of the solo part that is accepted by pianists without question? I suspect that it was Johann André, who brought out the first edition of the work, in parts, in 1794. For the most part, this version is extremely simple and not too offensive, but at times—for example in the accompaniment of the Larghetto theme—it is very clumsy, and the whole solo part would gain infinitely by revision and refinement in Mozart's own style. No other work—unless it be the score of *Figaro*—shows more clearly how badly we need a new edition of Mozart's works.[8]

Another *hors d'œuvre,* though in quite a different sense, is the Piano Concerto in B-flat (K. 595), Mozart's last, completed on 5 January of the year of which he did not live to see the end. He played it on 4 March 1791 —but not in an "academy" of his own, which the Viennese public would no longer support, but at a concert of the clarinetist Joseph Bähr, in the concert hall of the Court-Caterer Jahn in the Himmelpfortgasse (Gate-of-Heaven Road). Indeed, the work stands "at the gate of heaven," at the door of eternity. But when we term this Concerto a work of farewell we do so not at all from sentimentality, or from any misconception of this "last concerto for clavier." In the eleven months that remained to him, Mozart wrote a great deal of various kinds of music; it was not in the Requiem that he said his last word, however, but in this work, which belongs to a species in which he also said his greatest. This is the musical counterpart to the confession he made in his letters to the effect that life had lost attraction for him. When he wrote this Concerto, he had two terrible years behind him, years of disappointment in every sense, and 1790 had been even more terrible than 1789. He no longer rebelled against his fate, as he had in the G minor Symphony, to which, not only in key, but in other ways as well, this concerto is a sort of complement. Both these works, and only these, begin with a prefatory measure that established the "atmosphere" of the key, like the *Eroica* or a symphony by Bruckner. The mood of resignation no longer expresses itself loudly or emphatically; every stirring of energy is rejected or suppressed; and this fact makes all the more uncanny the depths of sadness that are touched in the shadings and modulations of the harmony. The Larghetto is full of a religious, or, as Mr. Girdlestone calls it, a "Franciscan" mildness; the

8. However, the NMA edition of 1960 still reprints André's version—though, to be sure, André's notes are carefully distinguished from Mozart's by the use of small music type. [*Editor*]

Finale breathes a veiled joyfulness, as if blessed children were playing in Elysian fields, joyful, but without hate and without love. Mozart used the theme of this Rondo a few days later for a song entitled *Sehnsucht nach dem Frühlinge* (Longing for Spring). The theme has the resigned cheerfulness that comes from the knowledge that this is the last spring. But the most moving thing about it is that in it Mozart received the divine gift of being able *zu sagen was er leide* (to tell the fullness of his suffering). This last Piano Concerto is also a work of the highest mastery in invention—invention that has the quality of that "second naïveté" of which we have spoken, welding the solo and tutti parts into the richest, closest relation, speaking in the most transparent sonority, and fusing perfectly the *galant* and "learned" styles. It is so perfect that the question of style has become meaningless. The very act of parting from life achieves immortality.

DONALD FRANCIS TOVEY

The Classical Concerto †

Sir Donald Tovey (1875–1940) was a pianist, composer, conductor, and musical scholar who spent the later part of his life, after 1914, as professor at Edinburgh. He published substantial studies of the Beethoven piano sonatas, the *Well-Tempered Clavier,* and the *Art of Fugue,* but he is best known for the miscellaneous *Essays in Musical Analysis* which were brought together in six volumes in the late 1930s. (The general title is a little deceptive, for in addition to some fairly detailed analytical essays, there are also some more comprehensive pieces, such as the one reprinted here, and many short program notes.) In the English-speaking world Tovey has been one of the most influential of twentieth-century musical analysts, second only, if at all, to his close contemporary Heinrich Schenker.

Tovey had a great knack of conveying a sense of the excitement of the many works he treated, and of interpreting technical details—notably those concerned with classical form and tonality—in esthetic terms. His musical sensitivity and insight were remarkable. Unfortunately, students may be put off by his famous eccentricities of style—his long digressions, sharp arguments with shadowy opponents, and provocative dogmatic assertions made without full support or explanation; *The Classical Concerto* has numerous examples. But these features should not be allowed to obscure Tovey's analysis and critical judgment of immediate musical issues. Few writers have had so much that is important to say about the classical masters from Bach to Brahms.

The Classical Concerto was written in 1903 when Tovey was twenty-eight. It is one of Tovey's most important essays, both intrinsically and historically, as an early episode in the twentieth-century "vindication of Mozart" referred to in footnote 1.

INTRODUCTION

Without a sound appreciation of those peculiarities of form which distinguish the classical concerto from the classical symphony the concerto

† From *Essays in Musical Analysis,* Oxford, 1936–39, III, pp. 3–27. Published by Oxford University Press; reprinted by permission.

can only be very imperfectly understood, whether by performers or by listeners; for the rational enthusiasm for great classics is the outcome not only of natural taste, but also of long familiarity with all that is purest in art; and so far as the opportunity for such familiarity is wanting, so far will current ideas and current criticism be vague, Philistine, and untrue. Now the number of great works in the true concerto form is surprisingly small; far smaller than the number of true symphonies. And of this small collection a good two-thirds has been contributed by Mozart, whose work has for the last fifty years been treated with neglect and lack of intelligent observation, for which we at the present time are paying dearly with a notable loss both of ear for fine detail and of grasp of musical works as definite wholes.[1] On the other hand, every virtuoso whose imagination is fired with the splendid spectacular effect of a full orchestra as a background for a display of instrumental technique has written concertos that express little else than that effect. Thus the name of concerto is assumed by literally hundreds of works that have not even an academic connexion with the classical idea of concerto form and style; while of the very small collection of true concertos the majority, those of Mozart, are ignored, and the remainder not nearly so well understood as any classical symphony. No composer attempts a symphony without a strong sense of responsibility, and some appreciation of the greatness of the classics of symphonic art, and so neither the number of spurious symphonies nor their tendency is such as to set an entirely false standard of criticism for the art. But that current criteria of the concerto are false, no one who seriously studies that form can doubt. The idea that the professed purpose of the form is technical display has been actually maintained by musicians who yield to none in their reverence and love for the great concertos of Beethoven and Mozart. Yet that idea is in flat violation of almost every fact in the early history of the form; and those who hold it seem to let it remain comfortably in their minds side by side with the opposite, and scarcely less untrue notion, that in the works of Bach and his contemporaries the solo part of a concerto is no more than *primus inter pares*. The first idea springs from the assumption (difficult to avoid, where bad works so overcrowd good ones) that art-forms are invented by bad artists to be disgustedly improved off the face of the earth by the

1. I do not know how many people in 1903 foresaw the vindication of Mozart, of which on the Continent the main impulse was given by Richard Strauss, and which dates in England from the memorable performance of the *Zauberflöte* at Cambridge some eight years after this essay appeared. That performance marked the first stages of Professor E. J. Dent's work upon Mozart's operas. [*Author's note of 1936*]

great men; and the second springs from the difficulty of recognizing in ancient art anything that does not happen to take much the same shape in modern art.

The only way to avoid these pitfalls is to seek out the typical artistic idea that is to be found in the concertos of the greatest composers. To avoid repeating what I have written elsewhere, I propose to follow out this train of thought in an historical, or at all events chronological, sketch, instead of applying it merely to any particular concerto. Opinions differ so much as to the way in which musical history should be written that I hesitate to call this sketch historical. Its object is to trace the successive forms in which what I shall call the concerto-idea has been realized. Those forms in which it has been falsified by vanity, or obscured by imperfect skill or vague thought, will not come under discussion at all, though to many historians that which is transitional and immature is often more interesting, and always more easy to discuss than that which is permanent and self-consistent.

To avoid a frequent source of misunderestanding, I must point out that neither here nor in any other of my analytical essays is the basis of analysis technical. It is frequently urged as an objection to all musical analysis that to investigate "how it is done" distracts the mind from the poetic enjoyment of a work of art. So it does; you cannot, for instance, enjoy the first movement of Beethoven's Eroica Symphony if you insist on thinking the while of Beethoven's seven or eight different sketches of its exposition. They are among the most wonderful documents recording the profound workings of a creative mind; but the only way in which they can help you to enjoy the symphony is by directing your attention to what it is. Follow up the sketches, then, as they approach the final version from something now more monotonous, now more violent, now smaller, now dangerously large, always changing with the surprising purpose and power of a creator who ruthlessly rejects all that will not remain as an inspiring force for all time, when what common admirers of genius call 'the inspiration of the moment' has gone the way of dreams and moods. Follow this up until it leads you to the ideal, the realized Eroica Symphony; and you will no longer think that there is anything prosaic in investigating "how it was done." But you will see this only if, as you listen to the symphony, you forget the sketches utterly, as Beethoven himself forgot them. They have helped you, not because they showed you "how it was done," but because they drew your attention to *what* was done; and on that, and that alone, your attention must remain fixed, or the whole object of all that loving and laborious sketching is lost.[2]

Musical analysis then is concerned with *what* is done. Unless the composer has left sketches, any attempt to speak of "*how* it is done" is downright charlatanry, a pretence of solving a problem that is beyond the human intellect. Beethoven himself must have found his old sketch-books a series of perpetual surprises if he ever looked at them a year or two after finishing a work.

An analysis that gives a faithful account of what is done in a work of art cannot but be a help, so long as it is not one-sided and is used in a practical way. Hence in my early essays I have aimed at quoting or at least metioning every theme in the works analysed, so that the material may lie conveniently before the eye. On the other hand, I have from the outset abandoned any attempt to confine the letterpress to what can be read in the concert-room. Quotations in musical type can be seen while they are heard; but the kind of prose explanation that can be read while the music is going on is as useless in the concert-room as it is at home.

Lastly, as this is an essay on a musical subject I have tried to treat it from a musical point of view. This again is not a limitation to technical matters; music is music, and does not become technical as soon as it is not discussed as if it were a nondescript mixture of intellect and emotion and poetry. As a plain musician I believe music to be music; poetry, a form of literature; painting, one of the plastic arts; and *all* to be poetry. But when I discuss music I shall speak of things musical, as beautiful harmony, breadth, firmness and depth of modulation, nobility of form, variety and contrast of tone, clear and well-motived contrast and harmonious fullness in those simultaneous combinations of melodies which we call counterpoint, for it is these things and others equally musical that make a concerto or a symphony what it is. And if it is objected that these things, as they occur in classical music, are non-poetical, or mere technical means of expressing some poetic idea that lies behind them, I can only reply that, so long as music remains music, this poetic idea will only be attainable through these musical phenomena. Certainly a criticism or an admiration that scorns the musical phenomena does not thereby become poetical; on the contrary, the man who expects music to give him poetical ideas while he refuses to listen to it as music, will infallibly, if he looks at other things as he looks at music, value poetry for the information it conveys when paraphrased in prose, architecture for the problems it

2. These famous sketches are printed in Gustav Nottebohm, *Ein Skizzenbuch von Beethoven aus dem Jahre 1903,* Leipzig, 1880, repr. 1967. [*Editor*]

solves in engineering, science for its practical use, and in short, everything for its lower and more accidental qualities, and this is the very type and essence of the prosaic mind.

To sum up: I believe the classical concerto to be a highly dramatic and poetic art-form, having nothing in common with the popular and pseudo-academic idea of the form except a few misleading superficial resemblances. I therefore propose to illustrate the poetic and dramatic expression of this form by an analysis that has nothing to do with technique, though it will use any good technical term that may substitute a word for a paragraph; nor anything to do with *a priori* theories of absolute music which will apply equally well to absolute nonsense, though it declines to talk of poetry when its business is to describe musical facts. I merely attempt to describe what may be *observed* by any one really fond of music, who takes pains to study the works of great composers in a spirit that endeavours to understand the ways of minds other than one's own.

THE CONCERTO PRINCIPLE

The primary fact that distinguishes all works that have in them the character of the concerto style is that their form is adapted to make the best effect expressible by opposed and unequal masses of instruments or voices. Whenever in classical or indeed in any really artistic music, you find that an art-form is to be expressed by a mass of instruments (under which head we may for present purposes include voices), and that this mass inevitably divides itself into two parts that cannot without some embarrassing limitation or *tour de force* be made to balance each other: then you will assuredly find that the form has been modified so as not merely to fit those conditions but to make them a special means of expression.

Hence arises at least half of the prejudice which many fairly experienced lovers of music, and nearly all inexperienced students of composition, feel against the concerto forms. When our experience is no more than enough to give us a keen pleasure in following the normal outlines of an art-form, and in seeing how they give reality and inevitableness to the contrasts and crises of the music, then we are prone to resent any influence that modifies the form, and we do not stop to see whether the new form may not be as grand as the old.

That the conditions of concerto form are in themselves unnatural or inartistic can certainly not be maintained in face of the facts. Nothing in human life and history is much more thrilling or of more ancient and universal experience than the antithesis of the individual and the crowd; an antithesis which is familiar in every degree, from flat opposition to harmonious reconciliation, and with every contrast and blending of emotion, and which has been of no less universal prominence in works of art than in life. Now the concerto forms express this antithesis with all possible force and delicacy. If there are devotees of "absolute music" who believe that this is the very reason why these forms are objectionable, as appealing to something outside music, we may first answer that, if this were so, then neither Brahms, Beethoven, Bach, Mozart, Haydn, nor any person of so much calibre as Clementi, ever was an "absolute musician," or had anything to do with such a mysterious abstraction. And secondly we may reply that this dramatic or human element is *not* outside the music, but most obviously inherent in the instruments that play the concerto; and that, so far as such a feebly metaphysical term as "absolute music" has a meaning, it can only mean "music that owes its form, contrasts, and details solely to its own musical resources." As long as musical instruments or voices exist, there will always be the obvious possibility of setting one instrument or voice against many; and the fact that this opposition exists also in human affairs is no reason why music should cease to be "absolute" or self-supporting—unless we are likewise to reason that man ceases to be human in so far as his five senses are shared by lower animals.

We must now see how the classical composers, to whom music was music no matter how profoundly it reflected humanity, adapted their art-forms to this condition of the antithesis between one and many, or between greater and less. I hope to show that the distinctive mark of the classical work is that it delights in this opposition and makes it expressive, while the pseudo-classics and the easy-going, thoughtless innovators, though they continually try to use it, miss the point with a curious uniformity amid diversity of error, and find every special condition of a concerto embarrassing and uninteresting.

Let us take these conditions in their earliest and, in some ways, simplest form. It is no use going farther back than the aria of Alessandro Scarlatti, or, to keep to familiar examples, Handel, in whom the conditions are not appreciably more developed. The Handelian aria is a clear and mature, yet an early and simple art-form. It owes almost its whole vitality to the opposition and relation between the voice and the accompaniment. When Handel was at work it was already dying of conventionality. And on this point I must beg leave to digress.

Conventionality is generally understood to mean something vaguely to the following effect: that a device may occur a very large number of times, say five hundred, in as many different works of art, and yet be in every instance the right thing in the right place, and therefore good and not conventional; but that the moment it occurs a five-hundred-and-first time, it becomes conventional and bad for all future occasions; so that we are entirely at the mercy of custom and history in the matter, and must know whether we are listening to No. 500 or to No. 501 before we can tell if either is beautiful or conventional. Now, though this is the real basis of more than half the current uses of the term, no one will believe it to be true when it is put before them in this form. The real meaning of "conventionality" is either an almost technical, quite blameless, and profoundly interesting aesthetic fact, more often met with where art aspires beyond the bounds of human expression than elsewhere; or else the meaning is that a device has been used unintelligently and without definite purpose. And it makes not an atom of difference whether this use is early or late: thus the device of the canon is, more often than not, vilely conventional in the late fifteenth and early sixteenth centuries, and extremely beautiful wherever it occurs in Schumann and Brahms. So long as a thing remains the right thing in the right place, custom has simply nothing to do with it. Custom may help us to understand what might otherwise be distressing in its remoteness from our humdrum ideas; and custom frequently is an unmitigated nuisance, making us feel towards classical works as an overgrown choir-boy whose voice is cracking must sometimes feel towards the forms of worship which have become too familiar to impress him—but custom never makes good criticism or in any way ministers to the enjoyment of art, so long as it is allowed to dictate to us.

This digression was necessary here, because all the concerto forms show an unusual number of constantly recurring features, and it is of great importance that we should never be misled into estimating these features as conventional merely because they are frequent. Indeed, the really conventional composer abolished them long ago. After using them in a hopelessly unintelligent way for some centuries, he naturally concluded that what he could not understand was of no use to any one, and so he avoided them in the very same conventional spirit in which he had at first used them. The original composer is nowhere more triumphantly unconventional than when he chooses an old device because he knows its meaning, and applies it rightly, in the teeth of all popular criticism and current notions as to originality and genius. Let us see how far Handel and Bach bear this out.

The arias of Scarlatti and Handel (and, of course, all opera and oratorio writers between archaic periods and Gluck) obviously depend on the antithesis between a voice and an instrumental accompaniment. This accompaniment is generally conceived as orchestral; and accordingly (though the orchestra is not often very formidable except in warlike scenes where trumpets and drums are treated vigorously), there is almost always the contrast between the single voice and the chorus of instruments. In fact, wherever Handel is not either employing some special instrumental effect, itself of a solo character, or else writing merely for voice and figured bass, his usual direction for the top part of the accompaniment is 'tutti unisoni'. But in any case the relation between voices and instruments is such that, as Gevaert teaches in his works on instrumentation, as soon as the living utterance of the voice strikes upon the ear, the orchestra falls into the background. This natural phenomenon is too powerful to be obscured by any perversions of modern taste. The callous and stupid use of it ought to have no influence on us. It has no influence on great artists, though they often shock contemporary critics, who have no better criterion of vulgarity than that it is what vulgar people do. As long as we know too much of what vulgar people do, we shall be worried and misled by the fact that, among other things, they ape their betters. Let us study their betters.

In great music, then, we may expect that such a contrast as that between a voice and an orchestra will always have its original value, and will be more, instead of less, impressive as the range of the art increases. Now it so happens that there is in a lesser degree just that kind of contrast between the quality of tone (not merely the volume) of a solo instrument and that of an orchestra. The solo player stands out from the orchestra as a living personality no less clearly, though somewhat less impressively, than the singer. Hence there was, in the period from Alessandro Scarlatti to Handel, the closest affinity, amounting in some cases to identity, between certain vocal and concerto forms. If we could understand a beautiful Handel aria so as to have some idea, however incomplete, of that wherein it differs from his hack-work, then we may hope to understand a Beethoven concerto.

When a voice or instrument is accompanied by something which it either thrusts into the background as soon as it is heard, or else fails to penetrate at all, a moment's reflection will convince us that the easiest way to give both elements their best effect is to let the accompaniment begin with a statement of the material, and then to bring in the voice or solo with a counter-statement. This arrangement brings out the force of the solo in thrusting the orchestra into the background, while at the same time the orchestra has had its say and need not seem unnaturally repressed as it probably would seem (supposing it to be at all powerful) if it were employed only to support the solo. Again, this ritornello of the orchestra, will, as its name implies, return its climax. The solo is probably more active, as well as more personal and eloquent, than the orchestra, and can therefore make a brilliant climax if it chooses; but it cannot make its climax very powerful in sound as compared with what the orchestra can obviously do with ease; and so this one missing element may be supplied, and the design rounded off, by bringing in the ritornello forte on the last note of the solo, thus ending the piece. Here we have the beginning and end of an enormous number of typical concerto forms. A single unbroken melody might be arranged in this way as a complete piece for a voice and orchestra, with no further elaboration and no other appearances of the orchestra except the opening ritornello and its recapitulation at the close; but generally the voice or solo goes farther afield and attains more than one climax in foreign keys, so that the orchestra introduces parts of its ritornello perhaps three or four times in such a movement.

Obviously much depends on the skill and sensibility of the composer in choosing different parts of this ritornello, bringing the solo into fresh relationship with it at each entry. Very early in the history of the operatic aria an important device was discovered, which is usually associated with the name of Alessandro Scarlatti. Its essential point is that the voice does not complete its first strain at once but allows the orchestra to finish it instead, and then begins again from the beginning, this time to continue.[3] The device obviously has great value in establishing a more subtle relation between voice and accompaniment than is possible when they persist in alternating only in large and complete sections. It soon became "conventional", that is to say a mere formula in the hands of composers who knew and cared nothing about the contrast and harmony of voice and accompaniment; and Mr. Fuller-Maitland, who describes it fully and accurately in the fourth volume of the *Oxford History of Music,* gives many instances of it in various stages of true feeling and decadence from Bach, in whose hands no device is more conventional than the very laws of nature, to Greene, who, in one of his anthems, shows its last trace in a

3. This device is commonly called the "motto beginning": see Donald Jay Grout, *A Short History of Opera,* 2nd ed., New York, 1965, pp. 105–08, etc. [*Editor*]

futile piece of mechanism lazily indicated by a da capo sign.

And yet the device has never died, aesthetically speaking, though we may not be conscious of its ancestry. Wherever a solo depends for its effect on entering after an orchestral ritornello, there we shall find the trace of Alessandro Scarlatti's principle—that the solo should first be inclined to enter into dialogue with the orchestra—the speaker should conciliate the crowd before he breaks into monologue.

I do not propose here to trace how Bach was influenced by his predecessors in this matter. Bach is an original composer, and no conventional ideas about originality will prevent him from using the most hackneyed device in its fullest and oldest meaning. His chief concerto form is in every particular derived from the typical vocal aria form, at least as regards the first movement.

A little consideration of the new conditions involved will help us to arrange the facts clearly. The opposition of solo and orchestra began early to take a greater variety of forms than was possible in the vocal music of the same periods. The main type of early concerto was the *concerto grosso,* in which the opposition was between such a number of solo players as could produce quite a complete mass of harmony to oppose against the orchestra proper. This opposition of the concertino against the orchestra or *concerto grosso* (from which the form takes its name) could even be reduced to a state of things in which all played together and split into whatever groups they pleased; as in Bach's magnificent Third Brandenburg Concerto, which is for a string orchestra which plays in three parts in the ritornello, and divides itself into nine by way of representing solo passages—no further indication of a distinction between solo and tutti being given. Still, apart from the likelihood that Bach was writing for only nine players, and that in performance by a larger band the nine-part passages should be played by the leaders alone, this dividing of the orchestra at once produces a fairly strong impression of that entry of individual tone which we know to be the most expressive feature of the concerto style; and this first movement of the only concerto throughout which Bach does not write for a detached solo-group or single solo, differs in no other way from the rest of his concertos.

We need only think of an aria enormously enlarged, with its square-cut melody turned into a concentrated group of pregnant, sequential figures, such as befit a serious and monumental movement that will not for a moment be confined within the limits of lyric melody. We shall find all the other features of the aria here: the ritornello, of course, states the main figures of the movement in their most forcible shape; then the quasi-solo of the orchestra divided into nine parts begins its version of the theme [m. 9], but, just as in Scarlatti's arias, bursts into a tutti [m. 12] before the phrase is finished, though the greater scale of the movement (and a higher organization in every respect) is indicated by the fact that this interruption is in a new key. Another interruption occurs [m. 19] before the resumed nine-part passages can deliver a longer sentence; and we have to go some way into the movement before these quasi-solos have any long uninterrupted discourse. Thoughout the work the principles of alternation between quasi-solo and tutti are most subtle and delicate in their adaptation to the peculiar conditions of this band. Sometimes the three basses coalesce into tutti while the six upper parts remain individual; in one most impressive place, the basses do this in order to bring out a difficult passage, thus retaining their value as solo parts [m. 114f.].[4] Sometimes basses and violins will each coalesce while the three viola parts flourish separately. In short, the combinations are endless, and are all in the highest degree expressive of the peculiar concerto opposition of forces. This is what Bach does under conditions in which the possibilities of concerto style are least obvious.

The Second Brandenburg Concerto is for four solo instruments and orchestra. Here the principles of the form are far more obvious. Yet they cannot be so strongly marked in a concerto for four instruments as in a concerto for one; and if Bach's extant concertos be studied as glorified arias, the vital aesthetic principles will reveal themselves in endless variety. (Incidentally these principles will help us to restore by conjecture the original forms of works extant only in arrangement.) Bach, far more than Handel, likes to organize both his larger arias and his concertos by making the solo enter with a different theme from that of the ritornello, so that when the orchestra breaks in on the first solo with Scarlatti's interruption (or something to that effect) the bit of ritornello so introduced has a new meaning. Sometimes he translates into these larger instrumental forms the things that happen in an aria where a solo instrument as well as a voice is opposed to the orchestra. Further details must be left to other analyses of Bach's vocal and instrumental works. Here we can only add that Bach, like the masters of later concerto forms, makes the relation of solo and tutti more intimate and less contrasted in middle and final than in first movements.

4. For Tovey's essay on the Brandenburg Concerto No. 3, see *Essays in Musical Analysis*, II, pp. 190–93. [*Editor*]

In short, Bach's concerto forms are completely identical with his vocal forms, except those that are dramatic, like some of Handel's, and those that employ the orchestra merely as a support, such as fugues and the severer forms of figured choral.

In the case of festive choruses, where form and brilliance are more important than fugue and solemnity, this identity is such that actual concerto movements have been arranged by Bach as choruses. And the arrangements are so amazingly successful that there is nothing but external evidence to prove that the chorus is not the original. The best illustration of this is the first chorus of a delightful cantata, *Vereinigte Zwietracht der wechselnde Saiten,*[5] written to celebrate the election of one Dr. Kortte to a professorship. The very title of the cantata throws light on the concerto idea; for *Vereinigte Zwietracht* is a singularly accurate and forcible rendering of the root meaning of *concertare*; and Bach generally calls the solo part (*Cembalo, Violino,* or whatever the case may be) *certato.*[6]

When we compare Bach's rendering of this "united contest of turnabout strings" with the third movement of the First Brandenburg Concerto, we find that the framework, themes, and counterpoint are bar for bar the same, with the exception of an occasional expansion (two bars inserted here, half a bar there), to make the approaches to climaxes longer and more suitable to the grander massiveness of choral writing. But what will strike us most forcibly is that the chorus parts are derived, not from the horns and other wind-parts of the original, but entirely from the single solo part, a struggling violino piccolo (Quart-Geige, or kit), that has more difficulty in getting the upper hand of the orchestra than any other solo in the whole classical repertoire. The transformation of this thinnest of solo threads into massive and stirring four-part choral writing is one of Bach's most astonishing feats of easy and unerring mastery. Any ordinary man would have reasoned as follows: "This movement is the only one in the concerto with a true solo, all the rest of the work being on the lines of the concerto grosso, and depending on the opposition of masses of string, wood-winds, and horns. And this solo part is not very brilliant, nor does it give me any material I cannot get more easily from the winds. Therefore I will either neglect it, or absorb it into the

5. Cantata No. 207. [*Editor*]

6. The true interpretation of this significant point is among my earliest recollections of that great musical scholar, A. J. Hipkins, whose kindness to me began in my childhood. [*Concertare* means "to contend . . . zealously"; Tovey's etymology is confirmed by David D. Boyden, *When Is a Concerto Not a Concerto?,* in *Musical Quarterly,* XLIII (1957), pp. 220–32.—*Editor*]

arrangement I propose to make of the wind-parts, which shall become the chorus. And now that I look at the structure of the movement, I see that there is much repetition caused by this tiresome little solo part, the motive of which will vanish when my chorus carries all before it. So I will cut out all these conventional repetitions, and make the form of my chorus free and terse." And so our *a priori* theorist achieves a breathless chorus in a jerry-built form. Thus the easy-going innovator (for all conventional minds are bursting with innovation) has arrived at the forms of many popular concertos of modern times. Bach's ways have nothing to do with *a priori* theorizing. In the true sense of the word he is the greatest of theorists, for he *sees,* he *understands,* and his vision is perfected in action.

Bach, or rather his chorus, seems to reply to our reasoner: "You complain that the violin part is overshadowed, and you point out that the rest of the work is a concerto grosso. But this first movement is not; and your complaint only proves that the violin arrested your attention from the moment it appeared, and made you wish that the orchestra allowed you to hear it better. The violin spoke to you like a voice, and you found it too weak; it shall become a chorus, and you shall learn that the whole orchestra always was its loyal bodyguard. The repetitions you think conventional shall continue to mean here exactly what they always meant —the transformation of a formal statement into the living and moving utterances of a personality; with this new splendour that the personality is that of a happy multitude inspired by one joy. The form of such a movement as this need no more change with a reversal of its balance of tone than the forms of the mountains change as the light falls at morning and evening. Let the horns become trumpets, let us hear the thunder-clap and roll of drums where the chorus sings of 'der rollende Pauken durchdringender Knall'; let the voices have more room here and there; but do not dream of losing the vital beauty that not only gives the movement its form, but is its very cause, the opposition of a *personality* to the impersonal orchestra. It is no matter whether that personality be an instrument, personal because isolated, or a chorus, personal because having human speech. The moment it appears it rivets our attention, and the orchestra itself becomes an eager listener expressing its sympathy in harmonious assent."

As if to demonstrate that the affinity between choral and concerto forms is no accident of an insensitive age, Handel once adapted some non-ritornello choruses (such as "Lift up your heads") into a huge concerto.[7] The results are abused enough to make the difference between right and wrong in this matter self-evident.

THE SONATA-FORM CONCERTO

We have seen how the early aria form was adapted to the conditions of a concerto; though we did not enter into many particulars about the aria itself. We must be more careful with the forms that underlie the concertos that are now to be discussed. The best way to avoid a tiresome abstract of ordinary sonata form will be for us to base our analysis on the difference between the sonata forms and those of Bach. The cardinal difference between sonata-style movements and those of the time of Bach is that the sonata movement changes on dramatic principles as it unfolds itself, whereas the older forms grow from one central idea and change only in becoming more effective as they proceed. Bach's grandest movements will show this no less than his smallest. You cannot, indeed, displace a bar without upsetting the whole; but the most experienced critic could not tell from looking at a portion out of its context whether it came from the beginning, middle, or end of the work. Yet almost any sufficiently long extract from the first movement of a sonata by Mozart or Beethoven would give a competent musician abundant indications of its place in the scheme.

It would be convenient if we could say that the polyphonic idea of form is the development of a single theme, while the sonata idea is the development and contrast of several; but it would not be at all true. The first movement of Bach's B minor Sonata for cembalo and flute has fifteen distinct figures—which is more than can be found in the extremely rich first movement of Brahms's G major Violin Sonata—and yet it is a perfect example of the true spirit of polyphonic form; while Haydn often gives us quite mature sonata movements in which it is impossible to find more than one theme. Still, the great thing to bear in mind is that the themes of the old polyphonic movement, if there are more than one, flow one into the other. The movement grows without ever showing impressive preparation for the advent of something new; and its surprises, many though they may be to a sympathetic listener, are never much connected with new themes or indeed with anything we do not seem to have known from the first. But a Haydn movement sets out in search of adventures; and if there is only one theme, that theme will somehow contrive

7. The concerto is the Concerto No. 2 *a due cori* in F (Handel, *Complete Works,* XLVII, pp. 169–75); "Lift up your heads" is a chorus from *Messiah.* [*Editor*]

to enter in another place disguised as its own twin brother. There will always be a vivid impression of *opposition* of ideas, and of change as well as development. And Haydn's frequent use of one theme where orthodoxy expects two is a result of amazing invention working on a deceptively small scale and seizing every conceivable means of making the dimensions of his work seem spacious, and its outlines free.

Hence the early instrumental forms were such that a short pregnant ritornello could sum up the principal material of a movement in a single line, while the solo was under no need to introduce more fresh matter than suited its disposition. But the material of sonata forms cannot be so briefly summed up; the ritornello, if it is used at all, must be larger and must contain more than one paragraph.

The great masters of sonata form were not to be persuaded to abandon the ritornello. The larger range of sonata movements, the treatment of the orchestra on lines as dramatic as those of the new forms, and the rise of a corresponding style of solo playing—all these facts conspire to make the ritornello more instead of less necessary than before. Bach's concerto orchestra was almost alway merely a string band; when he adds wind instruments to it, these show a strong tendency to detach themselves as subordinate solo parts; and so completely does he falsify the current idea about the parity of his orchestral and solo parts, that his great Double Concerto in C major for two cembalos reduces the string-band to a mere support, necessary and effective, but in no way opposed to the cembalos, who wrestle only with each other. Under these conditions Bach even abandons the ritornello. Not so the masters of sonata form: their orchestra uses wind instruments in every possible combination with the strings, sometimes opposed in groups, as in the old concerto grosso, sometime in solos, and constantly in perfect blending of tone with the strings as part of the compact chorus. Such an orchestra cannot be allowed to remain permanently in the background. On the other hand, the solo will need to be more brilliant than ever before, if it is to stand out against this orchestra which has already so much contrast of its own. The modern concerto form must rest more than ever on the old and natural concerto idea, the entry of a personal voice instantly arresting attention, and by mere force of its individuality thrusting even the most elaborate orchestra into the background. And the more rich the orchestra, and the greater the number and range of themes, the longer and more effectively may the appearance of this individual voice be delayed by an orchestral ritornello, if only this remains truly a ritornello and does not merge into pure symphonic writing. Here we have the key to the true method of conveying sonata form in terms of a concerto. The ordinary account of the matter, as given in standard treatises, is that the orchestra gives out the first and second subject with most of their accessories, more or less as in a symphony, but all in one key, instead of the first being in the tonic and the second in the dominant; that the solo then appears and restates these subjects somewhat more at leisure and in their proper complementary keys; after which there is a shorter recapitulation of part of the tutti in the new key, whereupon the solo again enters and works out an ordinary sonata development and recapitulation more or less in combination with the orchestra; after which the movement ends with a final tutti, interrupted by an extempore cadenza from the solo player. Now this scheme is, no doubt, rather like a concerto as it sounds to us when we are not listening; but it is falsified in all its most important particulars by nearly every concerto in the classical repertoire except Beethoven's in C minor; and the whole subsequent history of Beethoven's treatment of the form indicates that he learnt to regard the structure of the first tutti of his C minor concerto as a mistake.[8]

Let us try to discover the true concerto form by analysing a great work of Mozart, the Pianoforte Concerto in C major (Köchel 503), referring to parallel cases wherever they may help us.

Mozart begins with a majestic assertion of his key, C major, by the whole orchestra, with mysterious soft shadows, that give a solemn depth to the tone (Ex. 1).

The second of these sombre changes passes into C minor with extraordinary grandeur and breadth, and a new rhythmic figure (Ex. 2) rises quietly in the violins.

8. Tovey explains this point in his essay on the Beethoven C-minor Concerto, *Essays in Musical Analysis,* III, pp. 69–75. [*Editor*]

This new figure bursts out forte in the bass with a counterpoint on the violins (Ex. 3), in the major again, and with the full orchestra.

It modulates broadly and firmly to the dominant, which key it explores triumphantly, and finally annexes by trumpeting the rhythmic figure three times on G. Now this is not quite in the manner of a symphony. True, many of Mozart's earlier symphonic first themes consist, like Ex. 1, of little more than a vigorous assertion of the tonic and dominant chords; but they continue in a style that only slowly becomes more epigrammatic and melodious, and hardly rises to any surprising harmonic effect throughout the whole movement; whereas this concerto opening is mysterious and profound in its very first line. It shows at once a boldness and richness of style which is only to be found in Mozart's most advanced work. A symphony in this style would certainly begin with something more like an articulated regular theme, however openly it might be designed to emphasize the tonic and dominant of the key. (Compare the opening of the Jupiter Symphony. The Jupiter Symphony is the *locus classicus* for an architectural opening, but it takes no such risks as the opening of this concerto.) These solemn procedures have much the effect of an *introduction.* That impression is somewhat modified as the music carries us out with its tide, and we realize that we have indeed begun a grand voyage of discovery. This cannot be an introduction that leads to something with a beginning of its own, but it must be a preparation for some advent; and we can best realize how grand it is if we try to imagine the effect with which a chorus might enter at this close on the dominant (end of the passage beginning at Ex. 3). The entry of a chorus, singing the psalm *Dixit Dominus,* would be almost perfectly appropriate; indeed Mozart's church music, which is mostly of an earlier period, rarely attains to such power and solemnity as this opening. If we turn to Brahms's *Triumphlied,* we shall find that the orchestral introduction, through not nearly so long as these first fifty bars, is not unlike them in the way in which it covers its ground and seems to be leading up to something. But of course a chorus thrusts the orchestra far more into the background than a solo instrument can. Our opening tutti must develop further, for the orchestra will not sound relevant if repressed by the feeble tone of a single instrument before it has stated several contrasted themes.

We have, then, paused on the dominant. Observe again that the modulation to the dominant is not like the normal early modulations of symphonies. Though, if taken out of its context, the close of this passage would seem to be clearly in G, yet it here sounds only like very strong emphasis on the dominant of C. True, in symphonies of an earlier period Mozart would have followed his close by a second subject in G; but the effect of doing so is always a little epigrammatic—the taking advantage of a natural emphasis on the dominant so as to turn it into a new tonic; and I believe that Mozart differs, even in his earliest works, from ordinary composers in seeing that the device *is* epigrammatic, whereas they only saw that it was convenient and obvious. But it certainly would not tell in a work in the advanced style of this concerto. The only way to prepare the mind for G major after this grand opening would be to go to *its* dominant and pause on that. But the present close in G (in spite of the F sharp and all the firmness and emphasis) has not taken our minds out of C at all. We feel that we are *on* the dominant, not *in* it. Again, if this were a symphony and Mozart wished to begin his second subject, or preparations for it, at this point he would be almost certain to plunge into a remote and quiet key, most probably E flat, rather than use the old colourless device described above. And it is interesting to note that this is exactly what Beethoven did in the same circumstances in his C major concerto, when he had not yet realized the difference between symphonic form and the form of the concerto-ritornello (Another reason for making particular note of this possibility of E flat will appear later.)

What does Mozart do? He remains in C; and this fixity of key stamps the introductory ritornello character of the music more and more firmly the longer it continues. Out of that Beethovenish rhythmic figure arises a quiet march in C minor, half solemn, half gay, and wonderfully orchestrated (Ex. 4).

This is repeated by the wind, with soft trumpets and drums, in the major. "Here," explains the believer in standard accounts of concerto form, "we evidently have the second subject, which the solo will eventually restate in the dominant." Wait and see.

After this counter-statement there is a delightful kind of Hallelujah Chorus (Ex. 5), which settles with majestic grace into a quiet cadence-figure (Ex. 6);

and the grand pageant of themes closes in triumph. Then the strings seem to *listen,* for one moment of happy anticipation. As they listen the pianoforte enters, at first with scattered phrases (Ex. 7).

These quickly settle into a stream of florid melody, which grows to a brilliant climax in accordance with the artistic necessity that the solo should hold its own by doing that which most distinguishes it from the orchestra, and should therefore be florid just in proportion to the amount of orchestral impressiveness.[9]

9. Hence the source of all our delusions as to the relation between the concerto and the bravura styles. A modern concerto *must* be technically difficult, because all the easy ways in which a solo can stand out against an orchestra are harmonically and technically obvious, being the elementary things for which the instrument must be constructed if it is to be practicable at all; and as the orchestra becomes more varied and powerful, the soloist must dive deeper into the resources of his instrument. Hence the concertos of Mozart are in general far more difficult than any earlier ones; those of Beethoven the most difficult of all except those of Brahms; while the concertos of the virtuoso-composers, which exist mainly for technique, are easier than any others, since whatever types of passage they employ are written on progressions schematic at best, so that they can in time be mastered once for all like the knack of spinning a peg-top; whereas the great composer's passages never take your hand where it expects to go, and can be mastered by the muscle only in obedience to the continual dictation of the mind. Mozart's passages are in this respect among the most treacherous in existence.

On the top of this climax the full orchestra re-enters with Ex. 1, on the same principle as the bursting in of the ritornello upon the first utterances of the voice or solo in the polyphonic arias and concertos. The impressive soft shadows of this theme are now beautifully illuminated by running passages in the pianoforte, which continues the theme in close dialogue with the wind-band. Ex. 2 follows, yet more impressive, thrilled with the rise and fall of pianoforte scales. Instead of leading to a triumphant outburst in the major, it is continued in the minor with very dark colouring and great breadth of rhythm, and culminates on the dominant of C minor, which the full orchestra sternly emphasizes with the rhythmic figure (*a*) 𝄾♪♪♪♩. .Here, then, we have another pause on the dominant, not unlike that which we had shortly after Ex. 3. What does the pianoforte do now? It quietly modulates to E flat, exactly as we saw that Beethoven was tempted to do in the opening tutti of his first concerto. And that modulation, which is a mistake in a ritornello [10] because of its symphonic character, is for the same reason beautiful when the solo has entered and established its relation to the orchestra. Here Mozart gives the pianoforte a new theme (Ex. 8) pervaded by that omnipresent rhythmic figure (*a*).

Ex. 8

This modulates to the dominant of G in a broadly symphonic style, thoroughly expressive of the intention to establish the new key with firmness. Contrast what we felt about the passage following Ex. 3. After dwelling on this new dominant with sufficient breadth, the pianoforte settles down into the second subject. This will come as a surprise to orthodox believers in text-books, for it has nothing whatever to do with Ex. 4, which seemed so like a possible second subject. Indeed the only part of it that has anything to do with the ritornello is a variation of Ex. 3, which obviously belonged originally to the first subject, though we may remember that the pianoforte had avoided it when it fell due after the solo statement of Ex. 2.

I need not describe the second subject in detail. Its new and main theme (Ex. 9) is first stated by the pianoforte—

10. I continue to apply this term to the whole opening tutti of the largest concertos. The longest opening tutti does not, if rightly designed, lose the unity that characterizes the true ritornello, even if it contains many important changes of key.

Ex. 9

and then counterstated and expanded by the wind instruments. The derivative of Ex. 3 follows (see Ex. 10) and leads brilliantly to a climax,

Ex. 10 (cf. 3)

with all that variety of colour and rhythm and continual increase of breadth which is one of the most unapproachable powers of the true classics, distinguishing them no less from the classicists, who do not know that they lack it, than from the romantic composers, the greatest of whom contrive to make their work depend on renouncing it in favour of epigram and antithesis.

On the top of this climax the orchestra, long pent-up, bursts in with Ex. 3 of the ritornello. And here Mozart contrives one of his most subtle and brilliant strokes. We saw that Ex. 3 originally led to G and closed emphatically in that key, but yet under circumstances that made us feel that we were all the time only on the dominant of C. But now, of course, it begins in G, and Mozart so contrives that it remains there, instead of going on to the present dominant, D, as it would if transposed exactly; and it ends with the *very same notes* for no less than ten bars, *as in its original occurrence,* but now, of course, with the strongest possible feeling of being *in* G, not merely *on* the dominant. Thus Mozart cannot even do a mere repetition without shedding a new light that could not possibly be given by any variation. There is no describing the peculiar and subtle pleasure this device gives. It depends on a delicate sense of key, but has nothing to do with the technical knowledge which enables us to name it; indeed, it is certain to be keenly enjoyed by any attentive listener whose knowledge of music is the result of relish for classical works, stimulated by frequent opportunities for hearing them under good conditions. On the other hand, it is quite possible that many persons skilled in the mechanics of what passes for counterpoint, and having at least a concert-goer's retrospective view of musical history, simply do not hear these effects at all.

The sense of key-perspective can never be made obsolete by new harmonic developments. In otiose styles, whether early or recent, it is in abeyance; but a genuinely revolutionary style is more likely to stimulate than obliterate it. Strauss's opening of *Also sprach Zarathustra* might almost pass for a paraphrase of the opening of Mozart's C major Concerto.

The orchestra ends, trumpeting the rhythmic figure (*a*) on G as a finally established key. The pianoforte re-enters, repeating the figure on the dominant of E. And now it goes straight on with the march theme (Ex. 4) in E minor, which is to furnish our development section. The concerto has been grand and surprising, leaving us continually mystified as to what is to happen, and now it takes shape.

This theme that so happily pulls the whole design together all the way back from its single previous appearance in the ritornello, now moves calmly through a long series of very straightforward sequences through various keys. But though the sequences are simple in their steps, they are infinitely varied in colouring, and they rapidly increase in complexity until, to the surprise of any one who still [11] believes that Mozart is a childishly simple composer, they move in eight real parts.

These eight parts are in triple, or, if we count added thirds, quadruple canon, two in the strings, four in the wind with the added thirds, and two of light antiphonal scales in the pianoforte. No such polyphony has occurred since in any concerto, except one passage in the middle of the finale of Brahms's D minor.

Then there follows a majestic dominant pedal for the next eight bars, not at all polyphonic; the wind rises in a scale which the pianoforte crosses in descent, and just at the most satisfactory moment the full orchestra enters with the opening theme, Ex. 1; and we find ourselves in the recapitulation. The pianoforte shares the continuation, as in its first solo, and proceeds without alteration through the expanded version of Ex. 2 to the E flat theme, Ex. 8. This takes a new direction of very beautiful harmony and leads to the second subject. From this point the recapitulation bids fair to continue to follow its original exactly; but we find that the counter-statement of Ex. 9 is expanded in a new sequence of modulations in minor harmonies, and suddenly we find ourselves again in the broad daylight of the major key, listening to Ex. 4 as it was given in counter-statement in the ritornello! The pianoforte has a brilliant part of its own in this incident. Then the rest of the recapitulation follows, with Ex. 9 as if nothing had happened. And, of course, at the end

11. "Still": the reader must remember that this essay was written in 1903, at a time when Mozart was not widely appreciated. The passage in eight real parts is mm. 261f. [*Editor*]

the orchestra enters with Ex. 3, and comes to a pause on a $^6_4$ chord, whereon the pianoforte extemporizes a cadenza. After this the orchestra crowns the work with its final triumph of formal balance by repeating, what we have not heard since the first entry of the solo, the closing themes, Ex. 5 and 6.

It will be seen that this whole wonderful scheme entirely fails to fit the orthodox account of concerto form. Evidently the opening tutti has no connexion with the notion of a sonata exposition in one key; it is a true ritornello, differing from that of an aria only in its gigantic size. If further proof were wanted, Constanze's great bravura aria "Martern aller Arten" in the *Entführung* would furnish it, besides showing the use of auxiliary solos in the ritornello, a device revived by Brahms in the slow movement of his B flat Concerto. Of course there are plenty of cases where the second subject is represented in the ritornello, especially where the work is not on the largest scale; but there is no foreseeing what the solo will select from the ritornello. All that we can be sure of is that nothing will be without its function, and that everything will be unexpected and inevitable. I doubt whether three important concertos of Mozart (at least fifteen are important) could be found that agreed as closely in form as Beethoven's three greatest concertos (G, E flat, and the Violin Concerto). In one point they almost all agree, even down to the smallest works; and that is the splendid device of inserting in the recapitulation of the second subject a theme from the ritornello that was not represented in the original solo statement. In Beethoven's hands the concerto grew so large that this device would no longer be weighty enough to pull the design together, and so it has remained peculiar to Mozart.[12]

It is unnecessary to give a full account of the other movements; concertos, as they proceed, naturally use, like all sonata-works, more sectional forms, in which solo and orchestra alternate more simply than in the first movement. This is further necessitated by the fact that it can no longer be effective to lay such tremendous emphasis on the entries of the solo, now that it has so gloriously won its way into friendship with the

12. Further investigation will show that this device is the result of a larger principle which I had not grasped in 1903. The recapitulation in the tonic is a recapitulation of the opening tutti as well as of the first solo. It does not omit the features peculiar to the solo, but it adds to them those features of the ritornello which the solo had not at first adopted. In particular, it is likely to follow the course of the opening much more closely than in the first solo; and the subsequent appearance of a previously neglected theme is the most conspicuous result of this tendency. In Beethoven and Brahms the main principle is quite as clear, though it may not be marked by a special theme.

orchestral crowd. Hence the ritornello idea does not find such full expression in these later movements, though Mozart is very fond of using a simple kind of ritornello at the beginning of his larger slow movements, as in the present work. I give the three main themes of this ritornello in Ex. 11, 12, and 13.

The pianoforte turns Ex. 12 into a second subject and adds more themes to it; returning then by a really colossal passage on a dominant pedal to the main theme in the tonic, and a regular recapitulation of both subjects. Ex. 13 is reserved to round off the movement.[13]

Concerto finales are practically certain to be some kind of rondo. Mozart soon found out how to make the rondo form bring out the solo in the most appropriate way. He gives to the main theme (which is usually announced by the solo) a large number of orchestral accessories, which do not recur with the returns of the theme, until the very end where the solo shares in them as they round off the movement with fine effect.[14]

13. In some of Mozart's andantes, notably that of G major Concerto, the themes of the ritornello are so closely welded together that it is a great surprise to hear what we thought was part of one melody blossom out in a new key as a well-contrasted second subject.

14. Mozart found this use of accessory themes in the tonic valuable outside concertos. The finales of the two pianoforte quartets and of the great A major Violin Sonata are excellent examples.

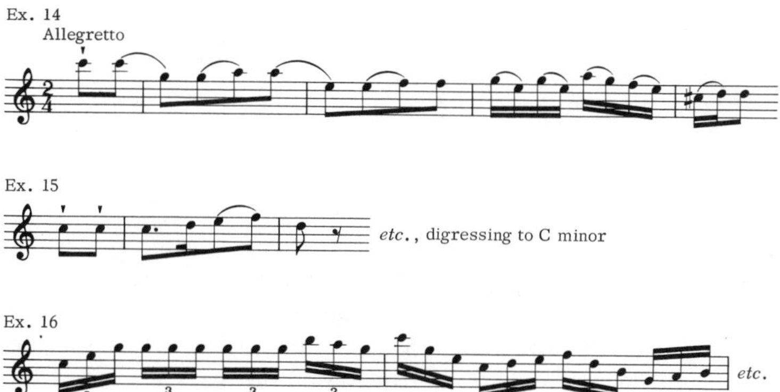

In the present instance, Mozart announces the main theme by the orchestra, and uses the accessories more extensively, making Ex. 15 modulate to A minor for the middle episode. But Ex. 16 appears only at the end of all, after a very big coda. In this finale the free-rhythmed connecting links between the main sections attain a breadth that was never approached until surpassed by Beethoven. Here are the remaining themes:

Ex. 21

CONCLUSION

Only the analysis of individual works can adequately show the later developments of the true concerto form. These chiefly concern the first movement; for the other movements are not much prevented by the special conditions of concerto form from growing on ordinary lines. But the following generalizations may be useful.

1. Beethoven ceased making the ritornello come to a full stop before the solo entered. In his three greatest concertos the end of the ritornello is dramatic and expectant, so that the solo enters on a dominant chord and ruminates in broad passages of immense dignity and beauty before taking up the themes. These passages correspond to the new theme with which Mozart so often begins the solos of his larger concertos; but, with their entry on the dominant and their non-thematic character, they produce a far more thrilling effect. Mozart's nearest approaches to this are in the concerto just analysed, in the much earlier A major Violin Concerto, where the solo begins with a short, florid adagio, in the brilliant and witty Pianoforte Concerto in B flat (Köchel 450) *** and in another big Concerto in C major (Köchel 467), where the solo enters on the dominant.

2. Beethoven did *not* "emancipate the orchestra" as is commonly held: he could not possibly have made it more prominent and elaborate than Mozart makes it in such works as that described here. On the contrary, he treated the pianoforte much more constantly in full harmony, and this inspired him with the possibility of accompanying it by very incomplete harmony in the orchestra and so producing numberless wonderful effects that can be heard under no other conditions.

3. Beethoven had the art of inventing themes which pass continually through several keys. This enabled him to give the opening tutti of his G major Concerto great variety of tonality without becoming symphonic or losing its unity as a ritornello.

4. In the same work he secures the novel effect of letting the pianoforte begin, and making the orchestra enter *in a foreign key* with the next phrase, after which the ritornello proceeds on the orchestra alone.

5. In his E flat Concerto he discovered the possibility of a rhapsodical solo introduction before the ritornello.

6. In the same work he found out how to construct a gigantic coda out of a new recapitulation of the later themes of the ritornello, including even the entry of the solo. This removes the one real defect of the classical form, that it entrusts the organization of the coda to the player's extempore powers in the cadenza.

Brahms further developed the concerto form in the following ways.

7. He found a way of modulation that gives the ritornello more than one key, and this, not by a series of transitions (like Beethoven's in the G major Concerto), but by a real contrast of fixed keys, all without loss of the necessary unity and flow.

8. He enlarged the notion of a solo introduction and made it both thematic and rhapsodic, thus saving space in the ensuing ritornello.

9. He did not, as used to be said, score too heavily for the solo; on the contrary he is demonstrably lighter than Mozart; but he uses the modern pianoforte in order to add greatly to the volume of a big tutti.

10. He discovered that if the solo takes most of its material from the orchestra, the orchestra may take some fresh material from the solo; and thus he obtained many new contrasts.

11. He found out how to write a symphonic scherzo for pianoforte and orchestra.

Such innovations do not make a formidable catalogue, but they are the outward signs of spiritual forces that are not concerned in the gyrations of the up-to-date weathercock. In the classical concerto forms the orchestra and solo are so organized that both are at their highest development. The conditions of such a problem do not admit many obviously different solutions; and the concertos that abandon the classical form obtain their unlimited variety by being structures of a much looser and less ambitious order. They stand on their own merits, and can be defined only by individual analysis. Beethoven had no reason, for example, to despise Weber's *Conzertstück;* and later composers, from Mendelssohn onwards, would have seen no reason why it should not have been called a concerto. It is manifestly better than Weber's regular concertos; and composers may as well write the best music they can, without being worried by a terminology that would confine the word 'concerto' to a form which exists in hardly thirty perfect examples.

C. M. GIRDLESTONE

From *The Twenty-First Concerto* †

C. M. Girdlestone (b. 1895) is not a professional musician but was professor of French at Newcastle, England, before his retirement. He has also written a valuable study of *Jean-Philippe Rameau, His Life and Work* (London, 1957).

II. We meet again in the andante the same breadth of conception, the same spacious lines, the same sustained motion of the themes, losing themselves one in the other instead of splitting up into separate sections. We find the same calm, lofty inspiration, more tender, however, as is befitting, and without the shadows which the frequent intrusions of the minor cast over the first movement.

Its form is that of a sonata where the *development* has been reduced to a few bars of transition—a form occurring at all periods of Mozart's life but which appears to have attracted him particularly during these months for he has made use of it in three of his most spacious compositions: this concerto and the two string quintets of the following spring. A few examples of it were to be found in his early concertos but the only other one of the great period to use it was K. 459.

The andante consists of two halves, the second of which reproduces the first with superficial differences, preceded by a tutti containing the chief themes. It begins with a group of short phrases whose meaning does

† From *Mozart's Piano Concertos,* London, 1948, pp. 431–44. By permission of Cassell and Company, Publishers. First American Edition published 1952 by the University of Oklahoma Press. Appeared originally as *Mozart et ses Concertos pour Piano* (Paris, 1939). Most of Girdlestone's music examples have been omitted and replaced by measure references to the score.

not become clear for some bars. Repetition and variation play a great part within the group; bars 3 and 4 are a variation[1] of 1 and 2; 7 and 8 repeat 5 and 6, varying the run; 9 and 10 give out the same phrase on different degrees and 11 repeats it, linking it up with the concluding cadence. The whole is made up of two-bar phrases. But the feeling which inspires them is so homogeneous and their outlines, consisting in rises and falls, are so similar, that they make up but one *song;* within it, the subtle variations of rhythm are such that no monotony has yet been felt when the uniformity is broken by a third bar added to the concluding strain (mm. 9–12). The violins double in the first four bars; elsewhere, the main work falls to the wind instruments from one to another of which, with great care for colour, Mozart passes the different fragments of his theme.

Hardly is the theme complete when a rustling of semi-quavers in the second violins opens a fresh section. With alternations of loud and soft it lasts for four bars. Its outline takes us back to the concerto for three pianos where a very similar motif had occurred in the same place. Against this background there stands out a fragment which begins *piano* with the first violins and closes *forte* with the whole orchestra; like the previous ones, it is repeated, then extended by a long descending scale which leads, *piano,* to the depths of the G string whence, on the lips of flute and hautboys, the tune rises again and concludes almost at once (mm. 16–19). Whereupon the final strain unrolls its threefold curve in a dialogue where first fiddles, horns and bassoons answer the other strings, and to which the flute, doubled by the bassoon, adds one last touch (mm. 19–22).

Such is the essence of the movement. The greater part of this tutti reappears in each of the two halves, with rearrangements in the scoring caused by the presence of the piano. In the first subject, only the horns keep their original part almost unchanged; the other instruments are excluded by the solo. The piano inserts its own theme between mm. 12 and 13; its rhythm is as diverse and as supple as the rest but it is more melodious and thus contrasts with the tutti where mass predominated over line. Not content with this solo, the piano takes over mm. 12*f* and, encouraged by the example of its fellows in the concerto for three pianos, appropriates the rustling accompaniment which suited the strings so well. It wants also to play the bass and, as its right hand is taken up with the trilling theme, the left hand part is rather heavy. The last frag-

1. This is not correct: mm. 1–2 (harmony: I–V) serves as an antecedent to mm. 3–4 (harmony: V–I) as a consequent. [*Editor*]

ment is extended by one bar and links on to a new subject which replaces mm. 19–22. This latter is certainly one of the queerest children of Mozart the melodist (mm. 51–53). It is an outline rather than a theme. Clearly Mozart wished to express something unusual and we experience at first the kind of surprise that we would like to be admiration, which overtakes us on hearing certain passages in Beethoven's late quartets.[2] But the mystery is cleared up when flute and hautboy, then bassoon, repeat it, modifying its skips, and the piano throws over it the graceful streamers of its scales and arpeggios (mm. 54–56).

The trill and C major close mark the end of this exposition. Between it and the reprise, instead of a *development,* there extends an ample transition which carries us back to F major, as in the andante of the C major quintet—a movement which gives us the feeling of expressing horizontally, in discursive melody, the mood that this andante expresses vertically and in mass. The transition is longer in the concerto and amounts to one seventh of the movement.

Its bass is a pedal on C, held at first by the strings, then by the horns reinforced later by the piano. It is an idealized example of those extemporizations on A with which organists enable an orchestra to tune up before a concert. Over this foundation the piano disports itself with happy majesty.[3] The movement's concentrated thought reaches its fullest utterance in the chords that follow this display of nimble energy; here, the effort, once scattered, gathers itself together; the introduction of the chords by the tutti causes their repetition in the solo to sound like a piano transcription of an orchestral passage. The solo instrument—the cantabile piano of 1780—recovers its true personality when it spins out their power in a flexible line of triplets whose wingspread ends by covering all the upper register and whose impetus flows over into the first bar of the reprise (mm. 68–74).

The recapitulation leaves out the solo subject and remains in the tonic; otherwise, it reproduces faithfully the first half of the solo. But the limits of the keyboard compel Mozart to modify the detail of mm. 51–53 [see mm. 94–96]. The movement ends with mm. 19–22; the woodwind

2. Girdlestone's puzzlement at this passage and his reference to late Beethoven quartets are hard to understand. [*Editor*]

3. The great leaps in the first bars must be filled in by the soloist; Reinecke's edition indicates upward runs between the dotted crotchet and the quaver; it is quite possible, however, to leave the octaves bare and insert the run on the way down, between the crotchet and the dotted crotchet. [For an early nineteenth-century solution, see pp. 98–99.—*Editor*]

give it out; then the piano and the other instruments repeat it with the original scoring, or nearly; the concluding upward scale in demi-semi-quavers belongs to the piano alone.

We have seen by what qualities this andante shows that it draws upon the same inspiration as the allegro. But certain features are its own and make it one of Mozart's most original slow movements. Despite its broad sweeps, its thought is concentrated; this is visible in the incessant changes of rhythm in the first and solo subjects, in the sometimes epigrammatic brevity of the other themes whose elements are always very short fragments repeated two or three times. We are conscious in it of a deep feeling which has some difficulty in uttering itself, and a good performance, while it should make the movement intelligible, will yet keep this sense of effort.

This andante, whose form is less easy to grasp at first sight than that of most of Mozart's movements, runs the risk of putting off executants, with its changing rhythms and its lack of sharply marked and melodious themes. It is most important not to hurry it; it is nearer adagio than andantino.[4] The expression of its dignity and breadth depends on its pace remaining even. The only place where a slight accelerando is permissible is in the solo subject, but a return must be made to the original speed with the rustling theme (mm. 43). It is especially disastrous to hurry the descending quavers in the first subject, which above all, should be *lasting*. The main difficulty lies in keeping the parts together; this once overcome, the rest will follow easily.

III. The finale is one of Mozart's most serious-minded rondos. Refrain and episodes have nothing of the merry tone of the usual rondo; one feels that the composer wished to end his concerto with a movement in keeping with the other two. We find the same breadth in the themes and their developments as in the allegro and andante, the same monumental conception and, in the mood, the same vacillation between certainty and doubt, expressed by hesitations between major and minor. The chief difference between this movement and the first is the absence of heroic accents; on the other hand, the middle couplet attains a degree of passion which has no counterpart in the allegro.

Mozart has gone five years back, to the ballet music of *Idomeneo,* to find his refrain. Its first eight bars reproduce almost literally the opening

4. We suggest ♪ = 100. [Einstein makes the same point: see p. 132.—*Editor*]

of the gavotte, transposed from G to C.[5] By omitting the *portamento* of demi-semi-quavers which, in the original, connected the first and second notes, he has made his theme less sentimental, but it remains none the less tinted with melancholy, serious, almost brooding, and full of a languishing grace unexpected in a concerto finale. It is only too easy to falsify its character, either by playing it too fast or by not respecting the phrasing which runs across the beat. The mark *piano* confirms the impression of gentle sadness.

The refrain is rather long and its plan irregular. After the gavotte itself, given out by the strings, the wind let us hear a march fragment, then the first violins repeat the last bars of the gavotte which seconds and violas complete with a cadential phrase (mm. 14–16). The 'cellos then do likewise, but in the minor, whilst firsts and seconds repeat mm. 14–16. The wind join in and after two bars the same phrase is repeated once more in the major. This passage is comparable to mm. 15–18 of the first movement—a restatement several times over of the same motif, in major and in minor, a device more typical of Beethoven than of Mozart, and very characteristic of this concerto. A short ritornello in the whole orchestra concludes this refrain in which the piano plays no part.

The solo instrument comes on with the first couplet [6] and the orches-

5. The Gavotte begins as follows:

See Hans Keller, *The* Idomeneo *Gavotte's Vicissitude,* in *The Music Review,* XIV (1953), pp. 155–57. [*Editor*]

6. I.e. the first episode in the rondo form. [*Editor*]

tra at once withdraws to the background. After an introductory theme, it launches out into a long and grand virtuosity passage where we notice the same care for varying the rhythm as in the other movements. It begins hesitatingly, like an unskilful walker picking his way gingerly in the midst of pitfalls (mm. 40–44). Then it grows more daring; the left hand engages in semi-quaver triplets, a formula which predominates in the piano part of this rondo. The strings mark the strong beats; the right hand punctuates the weak ones with chords, ending by taking possession of the triplets, and the music falls into its final stride, a firm, moderate gallop, whose majestic grace is in no way lessened by its impetus. The figure

is prominent in it. Soon the triplets pass back to the left hand; the right hand accompanies them while it converses with the strings and a short pedal on D announces the second subject which the piano gives out alone (mm. 75–83). As in the allegro, the wind restate it while the piano, still faithful to its triplets, climbs down and up more than three octaves with scales and arpeggios. The theme once enunciated, the solo enters on a magnificent transition passage, the most sustained and perhaps the grandest in all Mozart (twenty-two bars, 91–113). It is based entirely on a dominant pedal adorned by scales and fragments of arpeggios. The triplets remain hard at work; the orchestral accompaniment grows livelier. Towards the end, we enter the minor and the intensity reaches passion. At this point the whole orchestra intervenes and the wind weave a web of colour round the piano's untiring gallop (mm. 106–12).

The piano gives out the gavotte; the tutti repeat it *forte,* hammering out the last part. Then follow the little march and mm. 12–161 and 16f., but in this latter the 'cellos repeat the figure in the major and only [the cadential] fragment is in the minor.

The piano opens the second couplet—the *development* of the sonata rondo—with an aggressive theme [7] in A minor, the key in which we had stopped. The theme is repeated and is followed by a few bravura bars as a coda. As soon as it is over, three vigorous chords in the whole orchestra settle its fate and that of its key by removing us, without possible protest, into F major.

7. It is a transposition of the theme with which the piano had opened the first couplet. [This is Tovey's "middle episode": see p. 160.—*Editor*]

The piano now gives out one of Mozart's simplest and most personal tunes. At first sight, it seems almost inert, so calm is it. Many other themes of his are simple but usually their simplicity goes with ingenuousness; behind this one's reserve one feels the experience of maturity. It will be noticed that the true bass is given by the double-basses and not by the piano's left hand. Hautboys and flute restate it, decorating it slightly; the piano accompanies them with an "Alberti" figure; both this and the true bass differ from the bass lines of mm. 163–70.

The second part is more lively and the return of the triplets in the accompaniment betrays some restlessness (mm. 179–86). This time the 'cellos alone give out the bass. Hautboys and flute repeat the tune over the piano triplets, and here too there is a change. To express the gradually rising emotion, Mozart adds the warm tone of the bassoon to the double-basses. The advance does not stop at the end of the tune and we modulate quickly through a few bars into C minor. Thereupon the strings enter and oppose the wind and the piano accompaniment becomes more excited. We are on the threshold of the most stirring passage in the rondo.

What follows—a transfiguration of the French rondeau's *mineur*[8]—is profoundly dramatic. The pensive grace of the refrain, the calm assurance of the first solo vanish before a sorrowful and passionate conflict which carries us for an instant into the world of the last concerto. And, as so often happens with Mozart, the moment of the most poignant emotion is also that of the most complex and closely woven technique.

As in the *development* of the allegro, the kernel of the passage is a figure of a few notes derived from a theme already heard, and the working-out takes a contrapuntal form. As in the allegro, too, and indeed whenever Mozart combines closely instruments and solo, the woodwind are to the fore; the strings are reduced to sustaining or to keeping silence. Flute, hautboy and bassoon share the exposition of the drama. Once the key of C minor reached, the flute repeats the first four notes of [the F-major theme] which the bassoon takes up in a canon at the octave (m. 203).[9] The flute starts again and modulates to the dominant, G minor (mm. 204–6).[10] The hautboy gives out in its turn the beginning of [the theme]; the augmentation of one degree in the leap betrays heightened

8. I.e. the minor-mode episode that is a usual feature of the French *rondeau* form. [*Editor*]

9. We meet this figure again at the most dramatic moment (end of the *development*) of the B flat quartet, K. 589, first movement.

10. This is not correct; the flute figure merely moves to the dominant triad. [*Editor*]

stress. The flute replies with an imperfect canon at the fourth (mm. 207–10). Then the bassoon opens a further episode with a third exposition of the same fragment; the leap increases to an octave and the figure climbs swiftly from the bassoon to the hautboy and thence to the flute (mm. 210–13). As in the preceding episodes, the phrase is repeated, but this time, instead of passing on to the flute, the fragment returns from the hautboy to the bassoon (mm. 213–16) and the flute starts a last episode, the subject of which is still the beginning of [the F-major theme], but inverted, and moving downwards. The answers follow each other more closely and the threefold canon at the octave is compressed now into two bars (mm. 216–17). This episode, like the preceding, is given out twice, but nothing more follows; the orchestral part finishes *en echelon* as each one of the three instruments withdraws in turn (mm. 219–20). The basses hold on their fundamental G for two bars more; then, the piano continues alone and, in a long passage of broken sixths in triplets which drops and rises two octaves, the passion evaporates and the emotion returns to the level of the refrain.

Like all very dramatic passages in Mozart this one is short, but in every respect it is the most significant moment in the finale. Never had Mozart used the canon to express such passionate feeling. The growing intensity is perceptible, not only in the extending to a fourth, then to an octave, of the leap in the original figure, but also in length of the different episodes. The two first, in two-part imitation, decompose into periods of two bars each; the third is also in two-bar periods, but the counterpoint is now in three parts; it forms a miniature stretto. The overlapping phrases and episodes, the increase in length of periods and in number of parts, and the compression of the last episode, is exhilarating. No passage reveals more intimately the perfect union in Mozart between form and thought; in it we grasp admirably the manner in which one is at the service of the other, without either of them lording it. No passage shows better the meaning of the expression: to think, or feel, musically.

To round off the analysis of this fine *development,* we should say that all that follows the G minor modulation [11] is built upon a tonic pedal. In no work of Mozart are pedals as prominent as here.

And the piano, it will be asked? Has Mozart forgotten that he is writing a concerto and is he sacrificing his solo instrument upon the altar of his woodwind? Not at all. The lines of the design belong to them but the task of evoking the atmosphere, the impressionistic function, is the

11. See note 10. [*Editor*]

piano's. We have found in several concertos places where it accompanied a theme which was given out by the clarinet or the flute.[12] But here we have more than an accompaniment. The source of these bars is in the bravura passages of the concertos of John Sebastian and Philip Emmanuel Bach and their contemporaries, where the solo runs were punctuated in the strings by figures derived from the main themes. Already with the Bachs the orchestra's contribution was tending to become as important as the piano's; nevertheless, virtuosity remained the *raison d'être* of the passage. Here the centre of gravity has passed from the piano to the three representatives of the tutti.[13] Its presence is nevertheless indispensable. The waves of its triplets, breaking regularly bar by bar, fill out the slender lines traced by the instruments and punctuate each degree in the great ascent. This use of the piano for mass effects during a whole passage is new in Mozart for he is a conservative in this respect and, at a period when Clementi had been using it for some ten years in a manner resembling Beethoven, confined himself to a purely linear technique. We find similar piano writing in two almost contemporary sonatas: that in two movements in F, K. 533, at the end of the following year, and that in G, unfinished, for piano duet, whose kinship of style with this finale is such that Saint-Foix and Einstein both date it from this period.[14]

Only the gavotte is repeated at the reprise; however, the orchestra repeats it after the piano and thus gives the refrain a breadth unusual at this stage of the movement, where several other rondos leave it out altogether. This breadth is significant; it stresses the exceptional character of the stormy episode which has just closed. It raises in some sort a barrier between it and the rest of the movement which prevents it from contaminating the recapitulation and shows how foreign the normal nature of this finale is to such outbursts.

The third couplet repeats the first, abridging it; the beginning of the solo is omitted and the long bravura passage shortened. [The second subject] is given out in the tonic and the great transition which followed it is replaced by a new and briefer passage, which retains, however, the hesitations between major and minor; it also (mm. 301–2) contains a foretaste of the C major quintet.[15]

At the refrain's last appearance piano and tutti join forces. The re-

12. E.g. the finales of K. 482 and 488.
13. Who should play out, and *espressivo,* all through this passage.
14. K. 497a, composed in 1786. [*Editor*]
15. Allegro, mm. 270–72.

frain is given out entire; after the little march the woodwind are silent; the piano takes over the first violin part in (mm. 12–16), that of the basses and wind in (mm. 16–19), decorating them with gruppetti. It adds a rather long solo which it repeats; triplets preponderate in it and the writing recalls earlier solos; the orchestra stands quite in the background. After which, the tutti conclude the movement unceremoniously with the ritornello which had ended the first exposition of the refrain.

The problem with which a composer is presented in a concerto first movement occurs also in a finale when the latter's form is the sonata rondo: to wit, how to ensure that the last part of the movement shall be more than the mere repetition of the exposition. We have seen how Mozart solves it in an allegro. In most of his rondos he deals with it as felicitously as in his first movements. But here, the third couplet is really but a shortened version of the first with precisely the best parts left out. The coda consists in a long solo where virtuosity runs to seed and stifles the thought and the last bars repeat unchanged the commonplace ritornello we know already. As a result, the last quarter of the movement is frigid and we listen to it with some impatience. In spite of the general superiority of the sonata rondo, this is a case where the use of the two part rondo would have been more suitable. The dramatic central section does not dispose us to hear a second time what went before it; we would like to skip the recapitulation and pass at one bound from m. 229 to m. 308. Moreover, the coda, all in runs, is worthy neither of the finale nor of the work as a whole. It is clear that, after his superb *development,* Mozart had nothing more to say and grew tired of the work.[16]

This concerto is the last of the four that Mozart composed in C major. We have connected it with its 1785 predecessor and the string quintet which was to follow it a few months later, and, of course, the word Olympian, which we have used of it, evokes inevitably the so-called *Jupiter* symphony, although that work belongs more to the allegiance of Apollo than of Zeus. The key of C major, with those of F, B flat and D, is the key which Mozart has used most often; he is alike in this to all his contemporaries. Only, whereas the most used keys are not generally those in

16. Girdlestone's judgment of the finale is shared by Einstein (see p. 132) and Arthur Hutchings (p. 182), but not by Tovey, Keller (p. 195), or the present editor. This presents the student with a problem in criticism: he should ask himself whether the relatively unadventurous structure of the end of the finale really results in impoverishment or whether it may not serve a specific esthetic purpose. [*Editor*]

which he wrote his most distinctive works, some of his C majors do make up a well characterized family.

It is true that he used this key for many pieces about which there is little to say and, sometimes, in which there is not much to enjoy—works which reflect the personality of his period rather than his own. This is especially true of many youthful masses and symphonies, but also of many a sonata for piano, two or four hands, and for piano and violin, of late years.[17] The flute and harp concerto is no doubt the most successful of these drawing-room pieces since, whilst it keeps the impersonal exterior of the well-bred gentleman, it expresses something which is Mozart's own. But our concerto does not enter into this group.

C major is also the festal key, the key of pompous marches and overtures. It is the key with which he likes to begin and end his operas.[18] Used in this way, it often acquires strength and nobility,[19] and thus it becomes, in the last six years of the master's life, the key which expresses what we have called the Olympian quality of his inspiration. It takes by degrees the place of E flat which, at that period and down to Beethoven, is the essentially "heroic" key and was so with Mozart at the time of the *Sinfonia Concertante* and the wind serenade, K. 375. His first C major work where we recognize an unmistakable Olympian inspiration is the symphony K. 338 which he composed at Salzburg a year or two before his final departure. Later, he turned to this key for some of his noblest contrapuntal pieces: the fantasia and fugue, K. 394, the overture and fugue in the suite, K. 399, and above all the massive choruses of the C minor mass: *Cum sancto Spiritu, Sanctus* and *Hosanna.* We have noticed the same inspiration in the grand tutti with which the concerto K. 415 opened. We find it especially after 1785, spaciously expressed, in the family of works to which our concerto belongs: in the quartet K. 465, the two concertos, the quintet and the symphony. After this last work, he gives it up and returns to it only in opera; the overture of *Titus* is undoubtedly connected with the same stream of emotion as the concertos and quintet.

In spite of our strictures on the end of the rondo, this concerto is a very great work, one of the master's greatest. It is regrettable that, in the Mozart revival of recent years, the composer's trifling works should have received as much attention as his important ones, and even more. No one

17. K. 296, 303, 309, 330, 521.
18. *Die Entführung, Der Schauspieldirektor, Così fan tutte, Titus.*
19. Strength in the *Schauspieldirektor* overture, nobility in that of *Titus.*

can maintain that his best violin concertos are not heard as often as they should be, but who will dare say as much of the great piano concertos, far superior to those for violin, which count among the most valuable part of his creation? We know only too well the piano sonatas; those for violin are not neglected; but performances of the string quintets, the peaks of his chamber music, and of the three wind serenades, are still exceptional, whereas one station or another broadcasts every day the tiresome *Kleine Nachtmusik*.

With the concerto in C we reach the end of the period in Mozart's life when the concerto was his favourite means of expression. Two days after finishing it, the guard is changed and the symphony, in the person of the so-called Prague, K. 504, takes over duty. This taking over may even date from before the completion of the rondo; it is perhaps because the symphony he was composing had drawn all his vitality to itself that the conclusion of the concerto was so uninspired. However it be, hence forward the master's instrumental personality takes shape in the symphony and the quintet; other genres, including the concerto itself, survive as exceptions and none of them bear fruits as rich as those they have already produced. The period of his piano concertos is over.

HANS KELLER

K. 503: The Unity of Contrasting Themes and Movements†

A violinist and music critic, Hans Keller (b. 1919) is the most effective of a prominent group of postwar theorists in England who have been developing ideas of Rudolph Réti (1855–1957). Réti believed that one could demonstrate a unity, either direct or indirect ("latent"), among all the themes of a musical masterpiece. To him this was the only true field of musical analysis. Keller's discussion of K. 503 along these lines is very dense and often hard to follow, but the same has to be said of any really detailed music-analytical writing.

Réti's ideas are controversial and indeed obviously vulnerable, but they are also clearly symptomatic and build upon insights that were systematically ignored by analysts such as Tovey. The vigorous attack on Tovey in the present essay may be seen as a reflection of a broad generation gap, for Keller's thinking, despite its strong ties to nineteenth-century Darwinism, is also imbued with characteristic twentieth-century ideas that Tovey and Schenker simply could not entertain. The references to charismatic modern figures such as Freud and Schoenberg are significant: Keller's concept of "latent derivation" has a clear Freudian analogue, and his sensitivity to various rearrangements of note order (*e.g.,* inversion, "interversion," octave transposition) owes much to his study of Schoenberg, a composer whom Keller admires. Surprisingly modern, too, is a feature that disturbed many musicians of the 1950s, Keller's disregard for the normal temporal sequence of a musical work in favor of aspects of unity conceived of as independent of any time scale. This kind of thinking also underlies that type of contemporary music which "explores a sound-world" without reference to the traditional elements of sequence, implication, or musical cause-and-effect.

It may be suggested, in short, that Keller's article be read as one effort

† Reprinted from *The Music Review,* XVII (1956), 48–58 and 120–129, by permission of the editor, Mr. Geoffrey Sharp. With Mr. Sharp's permission, the British terminology of "crotchets," "quavers," etc., has been adapted to correspond to American usage.

(though by no means the only possible effort) to perceive the music of the past in ways that have been developed for the music of today, or yesterday. In this respect the article opens up what should be a central problem for the present-day student of old music.

PART I

> It is certain that . . . one can get beyond the instinctive faith in the great masters and account for one's finding something beautiful; this is doubtless necessary nowadays, if we consider how terribly arbitrary and superficial evaluations have become.
>
> . . . my colours follow from each other as of their own accord, and when I take a certain colour for my starting-point, I am quite clear in my mind about what to derive from it, and how to get life into it.
>
> . . . *Much,* indeed *everything* depends on my feeling for *the infinite variety* of tones *of the same family.*—VINCENT VAN GOGH, from the 418th letter to his brother (his italics).

Tautology is the greatest insult to the dignity of human thought. Yet most so-called "analytical" writing about music, from the humble programme-noter who has absolutely nothing up his record-sleeve to the great Tovey who may or may not have withheld a lot, boil down to mere tautological descriptions. I maintain that if you want to open your mouth or typewriter in order to enlarge upon music, you must have a special excuse. Mere "sensitivity," receptivity, and literacy will not do, for it will merely land you in describing the musical listener's own *perception* of the music, as distinct from promoting his *understanding*—whereupon, to be sure, he will consider you "an excellent critic."

> A succession of majestic chords in which the whole orchestra takes part opens the first movement. Built upon the triad of C major, they descend with slow stateliness from realms above, hastening a little as they draw near us, then rise again to beyond their starting-point.

Thus the much-praised Girdlestone[1] on the beginning of K. 503. This sort of "criticism" or "analysis" has two aspects, the descriptive and the metaphorical. The descriptive is senseless, the metaphorical usually nonsense. If you are so deaf that you don't hear that these C major chords (they aren't "built upon the triad of C major," but simply C major triads) "hasten" in the third bar (and not so "little" either!), I don't see that you will profit much by Girdlestone's assertion that they do so. And if you believe his metaphor that the chords "draw near you," "descending from realms above," you are so utterly stupid harmonically that,

1. C. M. Girdlestone, *Mozart's Piano Concertos,* London, 1948.

frankly, you aren't worth bothering about. The chords move away from home, and if "you" are anything, you are at home in the tonic triad: it is on the assumption of your capacity for *harmonic nostalgia* that the whole composition develops, and since the C major chords move the music away from the C major triad, they don't "draw near us." Not that all metaphors are of this kind. But in order to arrive at a psychologically valid metaphor, your musical understanding must be more, not less complete than it need be for some detailed technical observation, for only if you are omniscient about a particular passage can you ensure your metaphor against wrong implications in which any right point it may possess may be submerged. However, if you do know all that much, at any rate by way of your emotions, why not articulate your knowledge technically and thus save both yourself and the reader the trouble of analysing your metaphors instead of the music, in order to find out whether they mislead? What Girdlestone did, on the other hand, was to feel terribly sensitive and submit to the first wrong images that occurred to him, and to my knowledge everybody has submitted to his innumerable fallacies ever since. Once he got himself into the literary swing, of course, he could not get out of it: ". . . then rise again to beyond their starting-point." A musical child of six can see that this is absolute rubbish, but we nod our cultured heads in refined agreement. Who rises? The C major chords? But they are past and gone. Does, in fact, anything "rise"? "Then rise again" implies a motion corresponding to the previous "descent, with slow stateliness, from realms above," and there is no such motion. "Starting a tone higher, the same thing is repeated on the chord of the dominant seventh" would at least be a faultless description, if not so readable as Girdlestone's style.

Faultless descriptions are Tovey's speciality: his "analyses" are misnomers, even though there are occasional flashes of profound analytical insight. Otherwise, there is much eminently professional tautology. I have no doubt that Tovey was a great musician. His writings are a symptom of a social tragedy, for they are both a function of the stupidity of his audiences, the musical *nouveaux riches,* and too much of a mere reaction against the unmusicality of his academic forbears. "A new rhythmic figure rises quietly in the violins." Thus Tovey [2] on Ex. 4 (x [1]) below, in what has become a classical essay to which Hutchings refers as "a more penetrating analysis than will be found" in his own book.[3] But this isn't

2. In the essay reprinted above, p. 152. [*Editor*]
3. Arthur Hutchings, *A Companion to Mozart's Piano Concertos,* London, 1948.

analysis; it is pure pleonastic description. Anybody who has to be told this new rhythmic figure is a new rhythmic figure cannot possibly understand a bar of the Concerto, with or without Tovey's help.

> After dwelling on this new dominant with sufficient breadth, the pianoforte settles down into the second subject. This will come as a surprise to orthodox believers in text-books, for it has nothing whatever to do with Ex. [7], which seemed so like a possible second subject.

Is this analysis? Has anything been explained which we don't hear as a matter of course? According to the *Oxford English Dictionary,* to analyse means "to ascertain the elements of." Where are the elements of these new rhythmic and thematic entities? Where do they come from? How can they possibly be entirely new and yet be the inevitable consequences of what precedes them and the inevitable premises of what succeeds them? [4] If structural "analysis" does not show that, in a masterpiece, the new is not new, if it describes contrasts instead of analysing their unity, it is sailing under a black flag, pirating the music without paying anything in return. It is ultimately designed for the typical journalist's reader, who doesn't want to hear anything but what has been present in his own mind in the first place.

The analysis which here follows is based on the tenet that a great work can be *demonstrated* to grow from an all-embracing basic idea, and that the essential, if never-asked questions of why contrasting motifs and themes belong together, why a particular second subject necessarily belongs to a particular first, why a contrasting middle section belongs to its principal section, why a slow movement belongs to a first movement, and so forth, must be answered if an "analysis" is to deserve its name. During my work [5] on Mozart's chamber music as well as in the course of previous analyses, I have developed, first a method of analysis, and then, on a purely practical basis, a theory of unity, which I hope to formulate in full in a book on criticism. Frankly, I am in no hurry to systematize my abstractions: practice should precede theory. That, at the same time, I

4. This idea, introduced abruptly at this point and developed in the next paragraph, is at the heart of Keller's view of music. For Keller all musical elements in a masterpiece are "the inevitable consequences of what precedes them and the inevitable premises of what succeeds them," and the elucidation of this somewhat mystical tenet is for him the only true analysis. This is not exactly the same as saying that he regards everything else about music as unimportant; nevertheless, his writings necessarily give a one-sided impression of the musical process. [*Editor*]

5. Hans Keller, *The Chamber Music,* in H. C. Robbins Landon and Donald Mitchell, eds., *The Mozart Companion,* London, 1956, repr. New York, 1969.

continuously demand theoretical justification from myself goes without saying. But basically, my method is as intuitive passively as the creative process is actively, and from the reader I require nothing but an unprejudiced musician's *ear* which, as Schönberg has said, is the musician's sole brain. My analysis, then, aims at ascertaining the *latent* elements of the unity of *manifest* contrasts. Within the given space it cannot hope to be complete; I shall concentrate on the most difficult questions. I have not chosen the work to suit my own purposes; it was the Editor's choice. While I hope that my new approach is a proper way of paying homage to Mozart's genius, I hasten to qualify its newness and to draw attention to previous investigators and musicians to whom I feel indebted in some way or other—above all, to Oskar Adler and Arnold Schönberg; also, with certain reservations, to Heinrich Schenker and Rudolph Réti. I have detailed these acknowledgements in [the essay previously cited].

At the onset, I must ask the reader to keep the score at hand; my music examples are chiefly references: otherwise they would have to cover most of the work. The harmonic structure of melodic quotations must always be kept in mind. It will be convenient to regard the first movement's bars 1–7/1 [i.e. bar 1 through the first beat of bar 7] as the basic idea. I say "convenient" because strictly speaking, we ought to start from the opening, basic motif of the movement, but the derivation of what I call the basic idea from the basic motif [6] is obvious. The first problem is the contrast of Ex. 1 (bars 7 f.):

It is here that mainly conjunct melody takes over from the chordal arpeggio line of the basic idea. The contrast is thus twofold, melodic and rhythmic; it is thrown into relief by the texture, *i.e.* the contrasting orchestration, as well as by the dynamics and phrasing. Now, the melodic unity is afforded by the chordal progression from bar 4 to bar 5 which produces the central conjunct moment in the basic idea. Stripped of their respective rhythms, the violin (a) and flute (b) motifs containing this step reveal their antecedental significance for the bassoon and oboe phrases (c) of Ex. 1:

6. The basic motif is the fifth (tonic to dominant) expressed by the first three notes of the concerto. [*Editor*]

The derivation is one of "interversion"[7] *cum* transposition within a sequential frame: re-grouped and rhythmically standardized, the notes of (a) and (b) on the one hand, and (c) on the other, form a tonal sequence.

The rhythmic contrast is unified not only by the implications of the basic idea, but also by those of its background. On the one hand, that is to say, the dotted rhythm is already given by the basic motif, becoming more explicit in the timpani motif of bar 4 (diminution) and the first-oboe motif of bars 5–6 (augmentation), but these elements only establish a basis for the rhythm of Ex. 1, not the actual and specific unifying factor. On the other hand, however, it is easy to hear how a mediocre eighteenth-century composer would have constructed the opening passage rhythmically:

The unity of the contrast would thus have been more manifest, but the contrast itself would have been weaker. Mozart says: "Ex. 3 goes without saying, therefore, don't let's say it, but vary it immediately." I submit that this principle of composition, *i.e.* the simultaneous suppression and definite implication of the self-evident, pervades the music of every great master and, incidentally, makes the understanding of Schönberg's music difficult—because what was self-evident to him was not self-evident to everyone.[8] For obvious historical reasons, Mozart's terms of reference for suppressed backgrounds were more generally known.

The pulse of three eighth-notes which, with the dotted notes of Ex. 1, becomes near-manifest,[9] will prove a supremely important determinant

7. Rudolf Réti, *The Thematic Process in Music,* New York, 1951. [Réti defines interversion as "interchanging the notes of a thematic shape in order to produce a new [shape]" (*op. cit.,* p. 72).—*Editor*]

8. This "principle of composition" is another important tenet of Keller's, which is drawn upon repeatedly in the analysis that follows. [*Editor*]

9. "Pulse of three eighth-notes": *i.e.* the dotted quarter-note in m. 7, followed and pointed up by the pair of sixteenths, suggests a rhythm (pulse) of three eighth-notes. [*Editor*]

of the entire movement's unity. So far we have only been concerned with continuity which, as an aspect of unity, is comparatively easy to analyse. because the composer must always make continuity immediately convincing, at any rate on the emotional level, if the unfolding of his music is to be understood at all. As soon as we arrive at Tovey's "new rhythmic figure," [10] however, the question why the new is not really new becomes far more complicated; in fact, this contrast is perhaps one of the two most difficult to solve in the entire Concerto:

Its less difficult aspect is, of course, again that of continuity: I have added the preceding half-bar in Ex. 4 in order to make the transition from one motif (*cf.* Ex. 1) to the next, contrasting one more easily comprehensible. Melodically, the basic contrapuntal 2-bar sequence x^1 is an augmentation of x, derhythmicized to an extent which, to those who take a superficial view of classical music, seems characteristic of twelve-tone technique alone. However, the sequences continue up to G and then return to the tonic. Why up to G? Because the outline thus filled in, *i.e.* tonic-dominant, is but an "octave-transposed" version (to put it serially) of the basic tonic-dominant motif of the work.

Not that these factors would in themselves be strong enough to determine and define the unity: there must again be rhythmic and—since a "new" and surprising C minor has emerged—harmonic forces operating on a latent level. Once more from the standpoint of continuity, the latent rhythmic unity can be made manifest with comparative ease: the implied three-eighth-note pulse of Ex. 1 and of the first note in Ex. 4 comes to the fore in the upbeat of the "new rhythmic figure." The dotted quarter-note is split up into its constituent units: it is no chance that the three eighth-notes remain on the same note. Again, a mediocre eighteenth-century composer would no doubt only have been capable of a lesser contrast, interposing between Ex. 1 and Ex. 4 this kind of phrase:

10. At a later stage, he suddenly calls it a "Beethovenish rhythmic figure"—another deplorable instance of un-self-critically accepting the first association that springs to one's mind (compare Girdlestone on p. 177). Mozart used the figure far more often than Beethoven, and if Beethoven "had it" from anywhere, he had it from Mozart.

Ex. 5

Natural enough in itself, this phrase (whose rhythm is implied in the first bar of Ex. 4) would have amounted, in this context, to an obviosity. As I have tried to indicate [11], all masterly composition is compression: we may regard Ex. 5 as another suppressed background.

But it would be cheating to suggest that the rhythm of Ex. 4 has herewith been solved. Its three-eighth-note pulse is, after all, very different from that implied in Ex. 1: it has become an upbeat. In terms of continuity, to be sure, the new rhythm is implied by the implication of Ex. 5's rhythm at the beginning of Ex. 4, but this would again be too weak a determinant for so drastic a thematic contrast. Does the basic idea itself contain any implication of this upbeat?

The diminution of the basic motif's rhythm starts with the upbeat to bar 3, but this circumstance is only retrospectively realized, for when we hear the beginning of bar 3, the diminution has not fully established itself: it is defined by the middle of bar 3. In other words, rhythmic model and diminution overlap. Now, if we straighten out the rhythm of the diminution from where it is established, we arrive at the rhythm of Ex. 6:

Ex. 6

In the subsequent bar, this straightening process does in fact emerge to the surface, and it is again on the second beat of the bar that the new quarter-note rhythm is established. Consequently, the second, third, and fourth quarter-notes are invested with the significance of a three-quarter-note upbeat to the inverted seventh on the supertonic, and this three-quarter-note unit is confirmed, by way of counter-balance, by the first oboe's dotted half-note in bar 6. There is, then, the implication of a three-quarter-note upbeat in the basic idea, and the three-eighth-note upbeat of Tovey's "new rhythmic figure" is a straight diminution of it.

Even the C minor tonality, finally, which like the rhythmic figure itself proves of the greatest significance for the further development of the structure, is latent in the basic idea, *i.e.* in the flat sixth of bar 6.

"The only way to prepare the mind for G major after this grand

11. Keller, *op. cit.*

opening," says Tovey, "would be to go to *its* dominant and pause on that." And he goes on to give his famous explanation that since this does not happen, the close in G is "*on* the dominant, not *in* it." What he overlooks is that contrary to his description, the *Wechseldominante* [12] is in fact reached for a moment in bar 36, with the result that the close "on" the dominant is more "in" the dominant than it could otherwise be. In other words, the greatest possible harmonic contrast is established within the unity given by the close on the dominant and the ensuing, pre-determined C minor (see Ex. 4 and its harmonic derivation from the basic idea):

Ex. 7

The "new rhythmic figure" now appears in the shape of a chordal inversion or retrograde version (a) of the work's basic motif (tonic-dominant), but resumes the melodic line of its own first appearance (compare x^2 in Ex. 7 with x^1 in Ex. 4). The march character of this theme has been determined by the march character of the basic idea: note the extreme contrast which Mozart achieves within the *alla marcia* frame by a double-dotted march rhythm on the one hand and an entirely un-dotted march rhythm on the other. Soon, however, another dotted rhythm emerges as a counter-melody in the flute, not marchlike in itself, but, on the contrary, an almost lyrical *legato* syncopation—

Ex. 8

—whose rhythmic pattern proves to be a displacement of the rhythmic scheme of the basic idea's third bar,

Ex. 9

the syncopation itself being given by the basic idea's fourth bar (*et seqq.*),

12. *Wechseldominante:* dominant-seventh built on II, the "dominant of the dominant." Tovey might reply that certainly, the dominant of the dominant is "reached for a moment" as early as m. 31, but that neither here nor anywhere else in the passage up to m. 50 is the key of G major actually established. [*Editor*]

so that this semingly new idea represents a compression of two successive aspects of the basic idea. The ensuing march figure, again "new" on the surface level,

is based on the suppressed background of the basic idea (see Ex. 3) and, by way of straightening diminution, on the basic timpani motif (bar 4); while Ex. 12

proves a varied interversion of the harmonic degrees that make up Ex. 8's first seven notes. Motif (a) once more confirms the three-eighth-note pulse (upbeat) which had gone underground in Ex. 9, while motif (b) turns out to be a compression, harmonically varied, of the melodic cornerstones of the basic idea.

With the piano entry, the second of the Concerto's two most difficult problems of unity presents itself:

"The pianoforte enters," reports Tovey, "at first with scattered phrases. These quickly settle into a stream of florid melody . . ." But why are they scattered? How are they scattered? Why are they scattered in the way they are scattered? What, in short, is the compositorial cause of these absolutely unprecedented, utterly "new" triplets?

We have seen that various aspects of the three-eighth-note pulse have so far been exploited (Exs. 1, 4, 7, 8, 12); the triplet is its last and newest aspect. This circumstance makes the piano entry possible; it does not, however, necessitate it. There is only one conceivable *causa efficiens* for this drastically new rhythmic pattern: it must be a sharply implied variation of something which is the very opposite of new, *i.e.* something so self-evident that it has, again, been suppressed:

Ex. 14

This is the background continuity, more manifest two bars further along (*cf.* the rhythm of x in Ex. 13 and x[1] in Ex. 14). The shake is an extra-rhythmic device; the only possibility of defining it in the very process of its suppression is to vary it by another device which, in the manifest context, is "extra-rhythmic" too, inasmuch as it is without overt rhythmic precedent. The triplet alone fulfills this function.

The rhythmic reintegration with the three-eighth-note pulse must, of course, be all the more stringent. The basic manifest form of the three-eighth-note pulse is Tovey's "new rhythmic figure" (x[1] in Ex. 4)—in other words, a three-eighth-note upbeat implying a preceding eighth-note rest. We observe that the crucial triplets (Ex. 13, bar 2) start likewise with a (triplet) eighth-note rest, though for the moment a seemingly unrelated one. However, the next—and only other—triplets (built, of course on the rhythmic pattern of the 2nd bar of Ex. 13) retain the eighth-note rest (Ex. 15) which,

Ex. 15

meanwhile, has explained its latent significance, for Ex. 15 is, at the same time, a manifest variation of Ex. 16,

Ex. 16

whose derivation from the "new rhythmic figure" (x[1] in Ex. 4) is equally obvious and has indeed been consolidated as early as the *ritornello,* a few bars after Ex. 4:

Ex. 17

Melodically, the piano entry is of course based on the triadic opening of the basic idea, but what about the orchestral bar which introduces it? "Then the strings seem to *listen,* for one moment of happy anticipation." Tovey's perceptive metaphor, though completely valid psychologically, does not get us far below the descriptive level. A glance at Ex. 2 (a) and (b), however, does. We are again confronted with a motif consisting of the three conjunct degrees, mediant, subdominant, and dominant, that constitute the central entity of the basic idea. And now, in view of Ex. 2's own structural context, we realize how the opening of the solo exposition springs from the opening of the *ritornello* not only melodically, but also in its rhythmic-harmonic structure. Juxtaposing, that is to say, the suppressed background exposed in Ex. 14 with the foreground of the basic idea's continuation quoted in Ex. 1,

Ex. 18

we not merely hear the rhythmic origin of the piano entry, but actually detect a latent antecedent-consequent relationship between the two phrases. I have come to regard this principle of postponed complementation as a fundamental factor of unity in extended master structures.[13] For the rest, it may prove useful to remember that the way to a mysterious unity may easily lead over a hidden continuity.

According to Tovey, the theme of the bridge passage is again "a new theme," as indeed is its key, modulation to which would have been "a mistake in [the] ritornello because of its symphonic character":

Ex. 19

However true descriptively, Tovey's approach again fails to answer the most important creative questions. The point about this E flat major is that it *has* been reached [14] early on in the *ritornello* (Ex. 20), as a central, relative-major consequence of a C minor (Ex. 7) which, in its turn, we have heard to derive from the basic idea:

13. Keller, *op. cit.*
14. "Reached" but not established: *cf.* note 12. [*Editor*]

Ex. 20

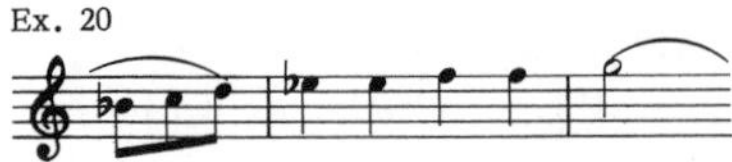

Rhythmically, the theme derives, by manifest continuity, from the rhythmic figure of Ex. 4 (x^1), the three-eighth-note pulse remaining operative throughout until, in the cadential phrase y^1, it confirms the relation of the theme with the opening of the solo exposition (see y in Ex. 13) on what one might call the premanifest level (on the analogy of Freud's preconscious system): upon reconsideration, Tovey could hardly maintain that y^1 was new, even in his restricted sense of the term; transposedly speaking, Ex. 13 (z) and Ex. 19 (z^1) are in fact identical. There are strong reasons for the theme's cadential re-emergence towards manifest unity with the solo opening; the melodic motif in question is once again that of the central entity of the basic idea (third to fifth degrees) (see Ex. 2 (a) and (b)) which, in the second part of this article, we shall hear playing a decisive part in the unity of the movement's principal contrast, formed by the second subject. Meanwhile, diving beneath the continuity of the three-eighth-note upbeat and pulse, we find that the 4 + 4 eighth-note pattern (second bar of Ex. 19) lies itself dormant in Ex. 4 (x^1), the change of notes on the latter halves of the first and third beats of the bar corresponding to Ex. 4's textural (imitational) change-overs at the identical metrical points. For the rest, the four-eighth-note unit is of course predetermined by the *ritornello*'s four eighth-note implication which I have made explicit in Ex. 5.

This predetermination assumes prime importance as soon as we come to examine the melodic-rhythmic derivation of the transition theme (Ex. 19). So far, we have traced back only the cadential phrase y^1—by far the easiest task. The preceding melody needs explanation, as does indeed the fact why the three-eighth-note pulse expresses itself in this particular way, why, for instance, the three-eighth-note upbeat assumes the melodic form of a group of two sixteenth-notes and two eighth-notes in bar 3. The answer can virtually be given without words. It is again a case of deferred complementation, and a little re-constructive re-composition will make the unity immediately clear (*cf.* Exs. 1 and 5):

Ex. 21

Behind this latent derivation, based again on the principle of the postponed consequent, there now looms the first-oboe (and violin) motif [15] of the basic idea which proceeds from the submediant to the dominant,

Ex. 22

touching on the way the very note which, as we have shown, is the ultimate source of the key of the present theme (Ex. 19), *i.e.* the flattened submediant. More "in front" of the creative causal chain are Exs. 8 and 12 with their rhythmic constituents.

By way of concluding this first part of our analysis, I would put forward a more tentative suggestion. I do not think that our interpretation of Ex. 19 (y^1) represents its ultimate reduction. It is, in fact, "too easy," too easily tangible. It may seem absurd to submit that something is implausible because it is too plausible, but the psychologist will understand my paradox, while the artist will at least be prepared to consider the proposition that in a composition which we call both masterly and "deep," every single contrast has as deep as possible a root of unity—deep enough, and therefore sufficiently concealed, to invest the contrast itself with the greatest possible intensity. The melodic outline of the basic idea's first phrase is given in Ex. 23 (*a*). Transposed to C major, the outline of Ex. 19 (y^1) is Ex. 23 (*b*), which turns out to be an interversion of Ex. 23 (*a*)'s notes (degrees), as well as containing, once again, the harmonic force of a postponed consequent.

Ex. 23

If this reduction is true, it applies of course equally to Ex. 13 (y) and indeed to the first bar of Ex. 13 which, we must not forget, is preceded by the C of the *ritornello*'s C major close. Particularly in view of the fact that a highly perfect cadence, emphasized by a three-quarter-notes' general pause, separates this C from what, according to our analysis, would be its background continuation as a melodic motif, we again have to assume, as (*inter alia*) in the case of Ex. 4, (x) and (x^1), that quasi-dodecaphonic de-rhythmicizations operate in classical music as latent unifying factors. I

15. In m. 6. [*Editor*]

have tried to show[16] that this is in fact the case: background serialism is, in my submission, a principle of classical unity.

The ultimate aim of the present method of analysis is to get at the heart of the music by dispensing with verbal accounts altogether. As soon as the principles of unity implied in the method are accepted, it will be possible to analyse unities simply by way of music examples (or, in lectures, by playing), with hardly a word in between.[17] There will be no more metaphors, no more pleonasms which, by their very nature, are always "sensitive": if you talk of a "false lie," you are sensitive to the fact that a lie is false.

PART II

As we have seen at the outset of Part I, the solo exposition's real second subject (Ex. 25 (*b*) below) presents what one might call the climax of Tovey's triumph over the text-books, "for it has nothing whatever to do with bars 51f. [*i.e.* Ex. 7], which seemed so like a possible second subject."[18] Ironically enough, the stupidest text-books are somewhat rehabilitated by our depth analysis. For so far as its unity with this C minor (later major) theme is concerned, the second subject illustrates once again our principle of postponed complementation. It would be cumbersome, though not difficult, to show why y in Ex. 25 (*b*) is a natural consequence of x in Ex. 25 (*a*) (which theme is, of course, immediately restated in the major), how the dotted mediant in Ex. 25 (*b*) is necessitated not only by the harmony, but also by the rhythm of Ex. 25 (*a*), including the upbeat and the eighth-note movement in the second violin. Fortunately, Mozart has done most of the job for us in a practical fashion. For once, that is to say, the latent compositorial background is, at the

16. Keller, *op. cit.*; also *Strict Serial Technique in Classical Music,* in *Tempo,* Autumn 1955 (but written after *The Chamber Music*).

17. Not long after this essay was written, Keller did in fact produce and broadcast "wordless functional analyses" of several classical compositions, analyses which consist simply of fragments of the composition and various reductions, "suppressed backgrounds," etc., played one after another in such a way as to show similarities and derivations. The quartet-score of Keller's functional analysis of the Mozart Quartet in D minor, K. 421, was published in *The Score,* No. 22 (1958), pp. 56–64. [*Editor*]

18. It did not seem so; it was. The second subject does in fact consist of two themes * * *: their exposition is split between the *tutti* and the solo expositions. The second-subject status of Ex. 7, that is to say, is structurally confirmed by the development and by the recapituation, where the two themes are united at the second-subject level, in reverse order. The following analysis proves that this uniting is really a reuniting process; as will be seen in Exs. 24–25, the manifest split between the themes corresponds to a latent split between their basic motifs which form a close background unity.

same time, a manifest historical background. In the second act finale (Ex. 24) of *Figaro,* which opera was completed on 29th April, 1786, *i.e.* about seven months before the completion of the present Concerto, Mozart confirmed our analysis by way of anticipation (see x^0 and y^0 in Ex. 24),

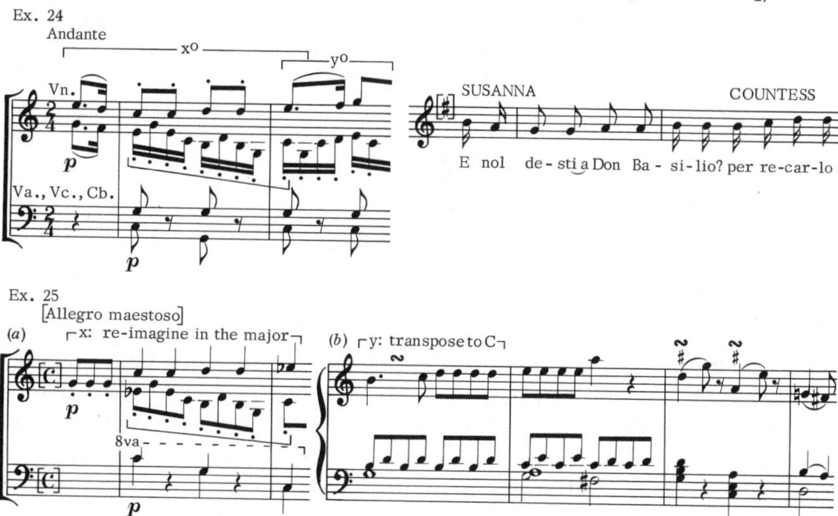

even going to the extent of showing that the melodic eighth-note movement of Ex. 25 (*b*) is an implied diminution of the quarter-note movement in Ex. 25 (*a*): see *"E nol desti a Don Basilio? per recarlo . . ."* in Ex. 24. Still further behind than Ex. 25 (*a*), there looms of course the suppressed background diminution brought to the fore in Ex. 5; in fact, the first thematic contrast of the piece (bars 7f., *cf.* also Exs. 1, 18, and 21) forms the antecedent for another deferred consequent:

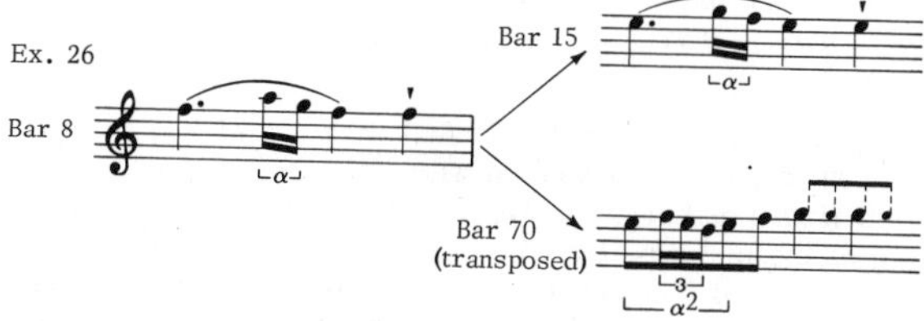

Ex. 26 even explains part of the determination of the second subject's motivic turn (a^2) as a developing variation of the two sixteenth-notes on the off-beat of the dotted rhythm (a). We have seen that bars 7f. derive from the central conjunct moment in the basic idea (bars 4–5, first violin on the one hand and flute on the other: see Ex. 2). So does, indeed, the basic phrase of the second subject (y in Ex. 25 (*b*)), which now furnishes the three conjunct degrees of both (a) and (b) in Ex. 2 in their proper scalic order (mediant, subdominant, dominant), thus reversing, at the same time, the orchestral bar (see Ex. 13) that introduces the piano entry; Ex. 27 takes the liberty of combining the two phrases:

"R" means, of course, retrograde motion. But there is another element of reversal here: we note that while the two phrases can go round in circles *ad infinitum,* the second subject's [19] makes a better unprepared beginning than the first's, *inter alia* because it is in fact an untransitional opening phrase upon the tonic root position with little of an "open" start, whereas the first's might be called an "interrupting cadence" which, if it is used for a start, *prepares for,* rather than *defines the beginning of,* a rhythmic structure: hear its introduction of the solo entry, where it hides the seams between *tutti* and solo.[20] The *later* (second subject) phrase, then, is more of an *ante*cedent, the earlier (first subject) one more of a consequent. The principle of postponed complementation thus manifests itself here by way of reversal—a process which I have often found to obtain in master structures, and which seems to me to contribute essentially to the build-up of background tensions over a wide musical space.[21] If, with my submission in mind, the reader will now cast his ear back to Exs. 8 and 12, requoted and reversed in Ex. 28 (B and A respectively), he will observe a pure and simple instance of this *"principle of reversed and postponed antecedents and consequents"* [22]:

19. By the second subject's "phrase" Keller means the first measure of Ex. 27, and by "the first's" (in the next line) he means the second measure of Ex. 27. [*Editor*]

20. It will be noticed that on rhythmic-harmonic grounds and for simplicity's sake, this analysis treats the beginning of the piano part as coinciding with the resumed first-subject stage. In precise reality, matters are, of course, far more complex: "the hiding of the seams," the transition between the first and the second exposition, is an extended process which includes the piano's first paragraph and ends with the *tutti* resumption of the principal theme proper in bar 112. This circumstance should be quite obvious on the descriptive level and need not detain us.

21. Keller, *The Chamber Music.*

22. *Ibid.*

In the movement itself, A is of course the earlier phrase, B the later one.

As for the second subject's turn (a^2 in Exs. 26 and 27) which, on the surface level, has emerged as an entirely new rhythmic element, Ex. 27 proves that it has a further determinant on top of a in Ex. 26, namely, Ex. 27's a^1—the very shake which, as we have noted in Part I, is also the determinant of the only previous rhythmic pattern of radical manifest "newness," *i.e.* the triplets in the piano entry (see Exs. 13–14).

How close is the integration of first and second subjects can be illustrated by once again reconstructing a suppressed background. Ex. 29 *(a)* gives the opening of the solo exposition, while Ex. 29 (*b*) recomposes it in the manner of a mediocre eighteenth-century musician (who has benefited from Mozart's art of transition), replacing the first- by the second-subject phrase; it will be observed that nothing else need be changed:

So far, however, we have not analysed the unity of first and second subjects beyond the latter's first bar (y in Ex. 25 (*b*)) which, based as it is on the tonic triad alone, does not yet show all the theme's distinguishing characteristics. The great surprise, in fact, comes with the second bar, both melodically and harmonically. The cadential leap from the submediant to the supertonic is something absolutely unique which removes the melody far from the "type" of which Girdlestone[23] considers it "the representative": the sudden disjunct motion arises out of the underlying function of a half-cadence—"quarter-cadence" would be the word!—to which the resolution of the third inversion of the chord of the seventh upon the supertonic is made subservient. It may indeed be said that the theme changes from the "melodic (conjunct) melody" of the first bar to the "harmonic melody" of the ensuing bars up to the imperfect cadence proper (end of Ex. 25 (*b*)): together with the opening turn, the basically harmonic, cadential skip at the end of the first two-bar phrase determines the entire melodic structure of the foreshortened second. But where do the harmonic determinants of this leap to the resolution's pivotal A come from in their turn? What, in fact, is the source of the second subject's harmonic structure?

When we turn to the authorities in order to find out what they have to say on the harmony of the first subject, we encounter a curious conspiracy of insensitivity on the purely descriptive plane; even the two leading writers, Tovey and Landon, are here thoroughly disappointing. The latter breezily talks of the beginning as of "a straightforward chordal alternation of I and V (or rather V_7)," and for Tovey, too, it is no more than "a majestic assertion of [Mozart's] key, C major, by the whole orchestra," "little more than a vigorous assertion of the tonic and dominant chords," even though a few lines further on we hear that the opening is "mysterious and profound in its very first line," that "it shows at once a boldness and richness of style which is only to be found in Mozart's most advanced work." But he does not explain this richness; what is less, his music example omits the C in the harmony of bars 4f., thus treating it as if it were a mere pedal. In Part I, it may be remembered, we have been careful to talk "of a three-quarter-note upbeat to the inverted seventh on the supertonic." The significance of what may have seemed a pedantic description should now become clear, for the ground-plan of the second subject's basic harmony—I–II $^{2}_{4}$–V $^{5}_{6}$–I—is identical with that of the first's, though the second compresses into two bars and a beat what the first subject had developed in no fewer than 16 bars: we have already indicated in Part I that all masterly composition is compression. For the more detailed textural relations between the two subjects within this common harmonic

23. Girdlestone, *op. cit.*, p. 427.

scheme, the reader is referred to the score.

In his preface to the Eulenburg pocket score, Friedrich Blume[24] remarks that

> one passage in the first movement remains obscure: bar 175 [second bar of Ex. 30], . . . 5th note, and bar 183, Flute and Oboe I, 5th note. In both cases the autograph reads a″ instead of a‴ (Oboe: a′ instead of a″). It might be that Mozart, with regard for the normal compass of piano[25] and flute at the time, deflected the motif in bar 175 downwards from sheer necessity (Beethoven did so frequently, but with Mozart cases of this kind do not seem to be known). But then there remains the question why he chose the lower octave also in the oboe. The parallel passage, bar 350, contains the motif (in lower position) in the piano part with the upward form[26] whilst in bars 358 seq. the flute and the oboe with the bassoon exchange both the upward and the downward version. Hence it is not by all means [*sic*] necessary to regard the downward turn in bars 175 and 183 as a makeshift which modern interpretation should avoid, and it is not cogent when older editions contain the higher note in this instance. Nevertheless the passage remains questionable. For this reason the upper note was given in small print in the present edition.

Musicologically, the passage is "questionable"; musically, perhaps it need not be. First of all, we observe that the second bar of Ex. 30

is not a mere variation of the second bar in Ex. 25 (*b*), but actually clinches the second subject's harmonic unity with the basic idea: the one harmonic element of the first subject which, since it does not occur in Ex. 25 (*b*), has been excluded from our above-defined ground-plan, *i.e.* the flat sixth of bar 6/4 [i.e. the fourth beat of bar 6] (Ex. 22), now reappears in a progression and compression strictly predetermined by the first subject itself. Now the quasi-serial octave transposition on which Blume ruminates is, of course, like all octave transpositions, a chordal inversion and therefore stresses the vertical aspect of our "harmonic melody" at what in any case is a crucial inflection, and what according to our analysis

24. The somewhat idiosyncratic translation, which is faithfully reproduced, is anonymous.

25. The piano keyboard of Mozart's time only went up to high F. [*Editor*]

26. "Upward *from*" in the actual translation: I hope I have resolved the misprint to the translator's satisfaction.

emerges as the conclusive point of definition of the harmonic unity between the two contrasting subjects of this sonata form. But Mozart wouldn't be Mozart if he neglected the melodic aspect of a principal motif while stressing its harmonic implications: as a matter of genius' natural course, he has composed himself into the only position where this *harmonic* inversion is identical with the *melodic* inversion, *i.e.* into an harmonic context where the octave transposition required is that of a tritone. In the recapitulation, this call to harmonic attention (which has been repeated in bar 183) is no longer necessary, so that Mozart can allow himself the characteristically paradoxical procedure of introducing the *straight* form of the motif *by way of variation.* Professor Blume's solution, then, is musically justified, whereas his doubts, expressed in the smaller-type note in Ex. 30, are not: the old editions are wrong.[27]

The rest of the movement does not contain any further problem of thematic or harmonic unity; we can safely leave it to the descriptive artists of musical criticism.

Nor do the other two movements show anything like the structural complexity of the first. I suppose this is what Professor Hutchings means when he says[28] that "had [the] second and third movements been as fine as [the] first, the whole work would have been a greater example of Mozart as a concertist than the so-called 'Emperor' Concerto is of Beethoven." But it is not legitimate critical method to turn the comparative complexity of successive movements with different functions into a criterion of evaluation; criticism's original sin is the lack of a *tertium comparationis.*

The principal theme of the *andante* grows from the basic idea and the second subject of the first movement, again by way of compression: the upbeat-bar, a descending tonic triad *arpeggio,* is melodically identical with bars 1/4–3/3 [*i.e.* the fourth beat of bar 1 to the third beat of bar 3], whence the phrase proceeds straight across to the other pillar of the basic idea and first subject, which made Landon speak of "a straightforward chordal alternation of I and V", *i.e.* the dominant seventh. And it is the leading-note in the treble that includes the second (solo) subject in

27. Many readers will find Keller's discussion of this point overingenious, as well as opaque. As for the "old editions," the *oldest* editions and manuscripts have no trace of the high As in m. 175 or m. 183, as is made clear by the Critical Notes for the NMA. [*Editor*]

28. Hutchings, *op. cit.*

this process of compression, for if you apply the parallel condensation of harmonic structure there and jump across to the dominant in root position (concluding half-cadence in Ex. 25 (*b*)), you hear the leading-note preceded by the tonic in the melody. In other words, the third note of the present theme is over-determined by the first and second subjects because it forms the pivot of their compression: we are dealing, as it were, with a background "modulation" from one melody into another.

The most difficult problem of unity in this movement is, not unnaturally, the main second-subject phrase,[29] Ex. 31 (*b*), here quoted in the tonic version of its orchestral exposition. Both the minor-seventh and the quartal skip from the third down to the seventh degree seem absolutely new thematically. As soon as we listen to the phrase serially, however, it emerges as but a variation of the first subject's first consequential consequence of y^1.

Ex. 31

Serial listening means being prepared for de- and re-rhythmicizing and octave transpositions. By way of octave transposition, x^1 derives from x. Why now does y^1 skip two notes of y? Because the variation, whose construction is horizontally harmonic, only includes harmonic notes. Once again we see how octave transposition serves to stress the vertical aspect of a "harmonic melody" at the crucial point of harmonic variation: in Ex. 31 (*a*), the conjunct C and B♭ form part of the same (dominant) chord, but in Ex. 31 (*b*), these two notes, now sharply distinguished and articulated by the minor seventh, mark the progression from tonic to dominant. In both instances, there then follows tonic-dominant-tonic; the f′ of Ex. 31 (*a*) has, for the moment, receded into the position of an ornamentation (shake) which, on the manifest level, is retro-determined by the cadence initiated by the ornamented note; it is rhythmically required owing to the paradoxical, melodic and harmonic need for a sustained, yet fast-moving leading-note. The cadence of Ex. 31 (*a*), finally,

29. This phrase appears in F in the ritornello, and then in C in the solo section. Tovey and Girdlestone refer to it as a "ritornello phrase," but Keller calls it "the main second-subject phrase" for the same reason that he calls the march theme in the ritornello of the Allegro maestoso the second subject: see note 18. [*Editor*]

is harmonically retained in Ex. 31 (*b*); the melodic variation y^2 is a sequential consequence of y^1.

The piano's own contribution to the second subject (Ex. 32) contains a triplet which is *not* an augmentation of the thirty-second-note triplet in Ex. 31 (*a*)'s cadence (z), but an augmentation of the very first (upbeat) bar, whose triadic $\frac{3}{4}$ quarter-notes form the proper rhythmic model. Nevertheless, from the standpoint of continuity as distinct from that of large-scale unity, the triplet does, at the same time, form a variation (by diminution) of a differently accented three-note pattern, *i.e.* the three-eighth-note upbeat at the corresponding juncture of the preceding bar (beginning of Ex. 32): [30]

I call this principle of developing variegation, with which the textbooks do not acquaint us, that of *"polyrhythmic diminution."* [31] For the rest, the thematic evolution taking place between the opening of the movement and Ex. 32, as well as the three-eighth-note upbeat following Ex. 32, does not leave us in any doubt about the fact that the penultimate source of these upbeating three-note rhythms is the three-eighth-note upbeat that plays such a basic rôle in the first movement (see, for instance, Ex. 4), while their ultimate source is the three-quarter-note upbeat which, in Part I, we have shown to be implied in the basic idea of the work.

What, on the other hand, *is* a "polyrhythmic augmentation" of z in Ex. 31 (*a*) is z^1 in Ex. 32: as in the case of the first movement, the two contrasting subjects emerge as two aspects of the same thought. At the same time, again from the point of view of continuity, the descending fourth with which Ex. 32 (as indeed the Concerto) opens proves basic

30. In m. 2 of Ex. 32, the right-hand chord A, F-sharp is a possible reading of Mozart's autograph; this reading is accepted in the Eulenburg edition which Keller is following, but rejected by the NMA. [*Editor*]

31. See Keller, *The Chamber Music.*

throughout the melody: z^1 is a sequential diminution of z^0 which, in its turn, applies the process of polyrhythmic diminution to the preceding bar. Ex. 33, then, extracts the fate of the fourth right to the end of the theme,

Ex. 33

which is followed by Ex. 31 (*b*) (in the dominant, of course), whose y^1 and y^2 emerge as the natural consequence of Ex. 33 as well as being, by dint of the orchestral exposition, one of its causes. Thus does continuity lead us back to the virtuous circle of unity.

In a previous *Music Review*,[32] I have already analysed the unity of the finale's chief thematic contrasts, including, of course, the central, subdominant episode. This analysis would have to be inserted in a complete version of our essay at the present stage, but readers of this journal would not, I feel sure, want me to waste their time and my space on what they have read before. It thus remains to solve the most difficult problem of the movement's unity with the basic idea of the work. The derivation of the *rondo* theme from the opening movement's first subject will not prove unfathomable, nor will many attentive musicians fail to notice that the new middle section which Mozart inserts instead of the *Idomeneo* Gavotte's reveals a further facet of the *alla marcia* element in the first movement (see the latter's basic idea on the one hand, and Ex. 7 on the other), while the lavishly modified return of the principal section reproduces the basic idea's flat sixth (Ex. 22) as well as its consequence, the tonic minor. The real problem is the central episode itself: it is such an extreme manifest contrast to every preceding theme that its indirect derivation from the rondo theme[33] hardly suffices for establishing its relation to the whole work's basic idea. Ex. 34, then, proposes to elicit the strongest direct connection with the first movement.

Ex. 34

(*a*) I, 19-20

32. Hans Keller, *The* Idomeneo *Gavotte's Vicissitude,* in *The Music Review,* XIV/2 (1953).

33. *Ibid.*

The unity between Ex. 34 (*a*) (*cf*. Ex. 4) and the basic idea has been analysed in Part I.

Bibliography

MOZART'S LIFE, WORK, LETTERS

Abert, Hermann, *W. A. Mozart,* 7th ed., 2 vols., Leipzig, 1956.
Still one of the best biographies and one of the two most comprehensive and authoritative studies of the works. It is a drastic revision of Otto Jahn's biography and was first published in 1919–21, as the 5th ed. of that work. The 7th ed. is essentially a reprint of the 5th; a third volume, incorporating corrections and additions, was announced as in preparation in 1955. There is unfortunately no English translation.

Anderson, Emily, *The Letters of Mozart and His Family,* 3 vols., London, 1938; 2nd ed., 2 vols., New York, 1966.
A selection from this work was published by Eric Blom as *Mozart's Letters* in a Penguin edition, 1956. Generous quotations from the letters are a feature of W. J. Turner's *Mozart, The Man and His Works,* revised ed., New York, 1966.

Deutsch, Otto Erich, *Mozart, a Documentary Biography,* transl. by Eric Blom, Peter Branscombe, and Jeremy Noble, Stanford, Calif., 1965.

Einstein, Alfred, *Mozart, His Character, His Work,* transl. by Arthur Mendel and Nathan Broder, New York, 1945.

Köchel, Ludwig Ritter von, *Chronologisch-thematisches Verzeichnis sämtlicher Tonwerke Wolfgang Amadé Mozarts,* 6th ed., Wiesbaden, 1964.
The celebrated thematic catalogue of Mozart's works, first published in 1862 at Leipzig.

Schneider, Otto, and Anton Algatzy, *Mozart-Handbuch,* Vienna, 1962.
Especially useful as a guide through the literature.

Wyzewa, Théodore de, and G. de Saint-Foix, *Wolfgang Amédée Mozart,* 5 vols., Paris, 1912–46.
This is the other comprehensive study of the works. Each one is examined in detail. The last 3 vols. are by Saint-Foix alone.

ON THE CONCERTO IN C AND THE CONCERTOS IN GENERAL

Badura-Skoda, Eva and Paul, *Interpreting Mozart on the Keyboard,* transl. by Leo Black, London, 1962.

Blume, Friedrich, introduction to the Eulenburg miniature score of K. 503, Eulenburg No. 774, 1936.

Freeman, Robert, *Mozart's Cadenzas for the Piano Concertos,* to appear in *Mozart-Jahrbuch.*

Gerstenberg, W., *Zum Autograph des Klavierkonzerts KV 503 (C-Dur),* in *Mozart-Jahrbuch 1953,* pp. 38–46.
Prints mm. 1–127 of the *Allegro maestoso* in Mozart's original "composition draft" or short-score version.

Hutchings, Arthur, *A Companion to Mozart's Piano Concertos,* London, 1948.
A book of the same type as, but inferior to, Girdlestone's *Mozart's Piano Concertos.*

Landon, H. C. Robbins, *The Concertos: (2) Their Musical Origin and Development,* in *The Mozart Companion,* ed. by H. C. Robbins Landon and Donald Mitchell, London, 1965, pp. 234–79.

Simon, Edwin J., *The Double Exposition in the Classic Concerto,* in *Journal of the American Musicological Society,* X (1957), 111–18.

* * *

Since the late 1930s, recordings of the Concerto in C have been made by the following pianists, among others: Kathleen Long, Gaby Casadesus, Edwin Fischer, Walter Gieseking, Rudolf Serkin, Leon Fleisher, Alfred Brendel, and Daniel Barenboim. The discontinued recording by Serkin (with the Columbia Symphony Orchestra, George Szell, cond.: Columbia ML 5169) was excellent. The inexpensive recording by Brendel is highly recommended for the solo performance (with the Pro Musica Orchestra, Vienna, Paul Angerer, cond.: Turnabout TV 34829).

Joseph Kerman is Heather Professor of Music at Oxford University and former chairman of the Music Department at the University of California at Berkeley. He is the author of *Opera as Drama* (1956), which includes chapters on eighteenth-century opera buffa and the operas of Mozart, *The Elizabethan Madrigal* (1962), *The Beethoven Quartets* (1967), and *A History of Art and Music* (1968, with H. W. Janson). He has edited *Beethoven: Autograph Miscellany British Museum Add. Ms. 29801 (the "Kafka Sketchbook")*, 1970.